中国思想文化术语多语种对外翻译
标准化建设项目成果
CHINESE THINKING AND CULTURE
MULTILINGUAL TERMINOLOGY DATABASE

中华源·河南故事
CHINESE CIVILIZATION
Stories from Henan

中原典故

ALLUSIONS OF THE CENTRAL PLAINS

河南省人民政府外事办公室　编

河南大学出版社
HENAN UNIVERSITY PRESS
·郑州·

图书在版编目（CIP）数据

中华源・河南故事 . 中原典故：汉英对照 / 河南省人民政府外事办公室编 . -- 郑州：河南大学出版社，2022.8

ISBN 978-7-5649-5308-9

Ⅰ . ①中… Ⅱ . ①河… Ⅲ . ①地方文化－河南－通俗读物－汉、英②汉语－典故－通俗读物－汉、英 Ⅳ . ① G127.61-49 ② H136.3-49

中国版本图书馆 CIP 数据核字（2022）第 162492 号

中原典故
ZHONGYUAN DIANGU

责任编辑	聂会佳
责任校对	刘利晓
封面设计	翟淼淼
版式设计	高枫叶
出版发行	河南大学出版社
	地址：郑州市郑东新区商务外环中华大厦2401号　邮编：450046
	电话：0371-86059701（营销部）
	0371-86059750（高等教育与职业教育分公司）
	网址：hupress.henu.edu.cn
排　　版	河南大学出版社设计排版部
印　　刷	河南博雅彩印有限公司
版　　次	2022年8月第1版　　印　次　2022年8月第1次印刷
开　　本	710 mm×1010 mm　1/16　印　张　10.5
字　　数	168千字　　　　　　　定　价　52.00元

版权所有，侵权必究。
本书如有印装质量问题，请与河南大学出版社营销部联系调换。

"中华源·河南故事"系列丛书编委会

顾　　问	黄友义	杨　平	范大祺		
主　　任	梁杰一				
副 主 任	卞　科	陈　岩	陈志伟	刁玉华	方启雄	韩国河
	惠　康	焦开举	介晓磊	孔留安	李冰冰	李　俊
	刘炯天	李向前	李　镇	梁留科	刘金锋	马萧林
	牛书成	牛卫国	屈凌波	屈鹏飞	史永庆	田　凯
	万正峰	王建修	王清义	王自文	许二平	杨建伟
	杨玮斌	俞海洛	张改平	张俊峰	张明超	张松文
	赵卫东					

主　　编	梁杰一				
副 主 编	李冰冰				
编　　委	陈国良	陈　玮	丁　锐	高　阳	徐恒振	郑延保
	孙立英	郭　远				

中华源·河南故事·中原典故

主　　编	屈凌波				
副 主 编	吴志远	钱建成			
中文撰稿	魏　涛	李晓敏	马伟华	田家溧	
英文译者	毛继红	李鸣翠	高诺丽		
英文审校	[美] Ronnie L. Littlejohn				
绘　　图	严　琰	姬凯平	殷琪萌	张　卉	任　雪	杨　姝

The Editorial Committee
Chinese Civilization
Stories from Henan

Consultants	Huang Youyi Yang Ping Fan Daqi
Director	Liang Jieyi
Deputy Directors	Bian Ke Chen Yan Chen Zhiwei Diao Yuhua
	Fang Qixiong Han Guohe Hui Kang Jiao Kaiju
	Jie Xiaolei Kong Liu'an Li Bingbing Li Jun
	Liu Jiongtian Li Xiangqian Li Zhen Liang Liuke
	Liu Jinfeng Ma Xiaolin Niu Shucheng Niu Weiguo
	Qu Lingbo Qu Pengfei Shi Yongqing Tian Kai
	Wan Zhengfeng Wang Jianxiu Wang Qingyi Wang Ziwen
	Xu Erping Yang Jianwei Yang Weibin Yu Hailuo
	Zhang Gaiping Zhang Junfeng Zhang Mingchao
	Zhang Songwen Zhao Weidong
Chief Editor	Liang Jieyi
Deputy Chief Editor	Li Bingbing
Editors	Chen Guoliang Chen Wei Ding Rui Gao Yang
	Xu Hengzhen Zheng Yanbao Sun Liying Guo Yuan

Chinese Civilization
Stories from Henan
Allusions of the Central Plains

Editor-in-Chief	Qu Lingbo
Associate Editors-in-Chief	Wu Zhiyuan Qian Jiancheng
Writers	Wei Tao Li Xiaomin Ma Weihua Tian Jiali
Translators	Mao Jihong Li Mingcui Gao Nuoli
Translation Proofreader	Ronnie L. Littlejohn (U. S.)
Illustrators	Yan Yan Ji Kaiping Yin Qimeng Zhang Hui
	Ren Xue Yang Shu

总　序

中国是世界四大文明古国之一，也是世界上唯一的古代文明传统未曾中断的国家。河南省地处中国中东部，是中华文明和中华民族的重要发祥地，在中国五千年的文明史上，河南作为国家政治、经济、文化的中心就长达三千多年。从某种意义上讲，一部河南史就是半部中国史。这里是中华人文始祖黄帝的故乡，是古丝绸之路的东方起点，是少林功夫和陈氏太极的发源地，这里创建了中国历史上最早的都城，镌刻了中国最古老的文字，诞生了中国最初的商业文明。

伴随着新时代的荣光，河南经济社会发展迅速，人民生活水平显著提升，这是河南人民自力更生、艰苦奋斗的历史结果，也是对外开放带来的益处。河南经济社会的发展、人民生活方式的改变都植根于深层次的文化积淀。为了让世界更多地了解河南，让河南更好地走向世界，2018年以来，河南省人民政府外事办公室认真研析了这片古老土地上的历史文化资源和时代风貌，组织各领域权威专家学者，编译了"中华源·河南故事"中外文系列丛书，选取黄河文化、河洛文化、老子、庄子、黄帝、少林功夫、太极拳、中医、汉字、丝绸之路、古都、农业、大运河、文物、陶瓷、青铜器、手工艺、书法、杂技、豫菜、豫剧、脱贫攻坚、空中丝绸之路、航空城、南水北调、中原粮谷、红旗渠、焦裕禄等多个主题，力图以故事的方式向世界展现一个立体、全面、真实的河南。

当今世界，人类文明无论是在物质还是在精神方面都取得了巨大进步，特别是物质的极大丰富，这在古代世界是完全不能想象的。同时，当代人类也面临着许多突出的难题，比如，贫富差距持续扩大，物欲追求奢华无度，个人主义恶性膨胀，社会诚信不断消减，伦理道德每况愈下，人与自然关系日趋紧张，等等。要解决这些难题，不仅需要运用人类今天的智慧和力量，而且需要运用人类历史上积累和储存的智慧和力量。河南历史文化底蕴深厚、包容性强，在今天仍极具现实意义。中原文化蕴含的思想智慧有助于修身养性，推动人类社会进步发展，焦裕禄精神、红旗渠精神所体现的为民爱民、艰苦奋斗的价值取向是构建人类命运共同体的力量源泉。我们期待与读者们一起从河南故事中汲取更多的智慧和力量，共同创造更加美好的未来。

Series Foreword

China is one of the four ancient civilizations in the world, and is also the only country in the world where the ancient civilization has not been interrupted. Located in east-central China, Henan Province is an important cradle for the Chinese nation and Chinese civilization. In the course of the five thousand years of Chinese history, for more than three thousand years it served as the political, economic and cultural center of the country and therefore, as generally accepted, represents half of the history of China. Henan is the native place of Yellow Emperor, the cradle of Chinese culture, the starting point of the ancient Silk Road in the east, and the birthplace of Shaolin Kungfu and Chen-style Taijiquan—typical examples of the world-renowned Chinese martial arts. It was here that the earliest capital city in China was founded, the oldest Chinese characters were engraved, and the earliest commerce took shape.

In the new era, Henan has witnessed rapid growth in its economy and remarkable improvement of people's living conditions owing to the national reform and opening-up policy and unremitting endeavors of the people. Modern economic achievements and social development as well as the changes of way of life could be traced back to its traditional values and cultural heritages. To enable people from other countries to understand Henan, and let the Province integrate more efficiently into the world development, the Foreign Affairs Office of the People's Government of Henan Province has organized teams of authoritative experts and scholars in relevant fields to compile this *Chinese Civilization: Stories from Henan* in Chinese and foreign languages since 2018 by crystallizing the excellence of traditions and outstanding features of modern development. The book series include *The Yellow River Culture, Heluo Culture, Laozi, Zhuangzi, The Yellow Emperor, Shaolin Kungfu, Taijiquan, Traditional Chinese Medicine,*

Chinese Characters, *The Silk Road*, *Ancient Chinese Capitals*, *Feeding the People—Agriculture*, *The Grand Canal*, *Cultural Heritage*, *Ceramic*, *Bronze*, *Handicraft Art*, *Calligraphy*, *Acrobatics*, *Henan Cuisine*, *Henan Opera*, *Poverty Alleviation*, *Silk Road in the Air*, *Zhengzhou—An Aviation City*, *South-to-North Water Diversion*, *Grain of the Central Plains*, *Man-Made River—Hongqiqu Canal*, *A Model Official—Jiao Yulu*, etc., presenting a panoramic picture of the Province.

In today's world, human civilization has made great progress in both material accumulation and ethical advancement, and the great abundance of materials today, especially, is beyond the imagination of the ancient people. At the same time, however, modern people are also confronted with a lot of problems, such as the widening gap between the rich and the poor, the indulgence in pursuit of luxury and extravagance, the undesirable extension of individualism, the decline of social integrity, and the increasingly tense relationship between man and nature. To solve the problems, we need to draw on the wisdom and powers developed today as well as those accumulated in the past. Henan is endowed with rich historical and cultural heritages characterized by its inclusiveness, and such heritages remain significant today. The intelligence and wisdom in Henan culture are conducive to self-cultivation and to the promotion of social development. The spirit of serving the people and relentless struggle, as embodied in Jiao Yulu and the man-made river—Hongqiqu Canal provides source of strength for building a community with a shared future for mankind. It is our hope that wisdom and strength from Henan stories could lead us to a shared brilliant future.

前　言

河南地处黄河中下游地区，是中华文明的主要发祥地之一。"一部中国史，半部河南史"的说法，形象地概括了中原历史文化在中华文明中的地位。从夏王朝到北宋的3000多年时间里，河南一直是中国的政治、经济、文化中心。在此期间，先后有20多个王朝在河南建都，200多个皇帝在此执政，儒学、佛学、文学、艺术等各种文化形态在中原大地上繁荣昌盛，难以数计的重大政治、军事、文化事件在河南发生。河南孕育了灿烂的历史文化，形成了一个蕴藏着丰富历史典故的宝藏。

据学者统计，发生在河南或者其他与河南相关的历史典故有数百个之多。每一个典故的背后，都有一个激动人心而又引人深思的历史故事。为了使读者更直观、生动地了解源远流长的中原历史文化，我们选取了其中最具有代表性的22个历史典故，按照先秦、秦汉魏晋南北朝、隋唐、宋元明清四个历史时期呈现给读者。这些典故绝大部分发生在北宋及以前，这也正是中原历史文化最灿烂辉煌的阶段。

纵观其中与文化相关的典故，可以发现中华文明的核心认知都在河南诞生、发展、定型。周公测影、杞人忧天的典故，反映了中国古人对宇宙结构、大地形状的认识，同时也见证了"中国"观念的产生。孔老问礼的典故，形象展现了中国古代最重要的两个思想流派——儒家思想和道家思想在中原地区的沟通交流。白马驮经，则反映了佛学从印度到中国落地生根的过程，凸显了中原文化开放包容的姿态。程门立雪、许衡不食无主之梨，则描绘了宋元之后最重要的儒学思想流派——程朱理学形成、传播的过程。

河南地处中国的中部，在整个国家政治、军事战略中占有重要地位，自古以来一直有"得中原者得天下"的说法。从东周时期楚庄王问鼎中原，到战国时期围魏救赵典故的发生；从秦汉之际刘邦、项羽争霸时楚河汉界的划定，到三国时期曹操老骥伏枥的雄心壮志；从唐代女皇武则天封禅嵩山，到北宋开国皇帝赵匡胤的杯酒释兵权：一幕幕影响中国历史进程的重大历史事件在河南上演。南宋以后，随着政治、经济中心的转移，河南渐渐衰落下去，相应典故的数量也随之减少。但中原文化对世界文明依然有所贡献，布衣王子朱载堉发明十二平均律就是其中最杰出的代表。

本书精选的历史典故，在注重趣味性、生动性的同时，着力呈现中原文化是中华文化主要源头和主干的特点，让读者从这些典故中了解中华文化整体的发展脉络，领略、感知河南文化和中华文明的博大精深。

Preface

Henan, one of the cradles of Chinese civilization, stands at the middle and lower reaches of the Yellow River. The saying "Henan's history accounts for half of China's history" is a vivid portrayal of the Central Plains' status in the history and culture of Chinese civilization. Henan remained the political, economic and cultural core of China for over 3000 years from the Xia Dynasty to the Northern Song Dynasty. During this period, a total of over 20 dynasties established their capitals in Henan, over 200 emperors governed here, and Confucianism, Buddhism, Chinese literature, Chinese art and other cultural forms blossomed in the Central Plains. Henan has witnessed countless major political, military and cultural events, nurtured dazzling history and culture, and created a treasure island rich in historical allusions.

According to statistics compiled by scholars, hundreds of historical allusions occurred in or are related to Henan. An impressive and thought-provoking story hides behind every allusion. To expose readers to long-standing history and culture of the Central Plains in a more straight and vivid manner, we have selected 22 typical allusions, which are presented to readers according to four historical periods of the Central Plains: ① The Pre-Qin period; ② The Qin, Han, Wei, Jin, and Southern and Northern dynasties; ③ The Sui and Tang dynasties; ④ The Song, Yuan, Ming and Qing dynasties. Most of these allusions occurred before the Northern Song Dynasty, a prime time of history and culture of the Central Plains.

The defining philosophy of Chinese civilization was born, grew and took shape in Henan and may be seen through a glimpse of the region's cultural allusions. The allusions of "Zhou Gong Measuring the Length of the Shadow" and "The Man of Qi Worrying About the Sky" reflect an ancient Chinese recognition of the structure of the universe and the shape of the earth, and also bear witness to the birth of the concept "China". The allusion of "Confucius Asking Laozi About Rites" vividly shows the mutual exchange between Confucianism and Daoism, the two most vital schools of thought in ancient China in the Central Plains. The classical story of "The White Horse Carrying Buddhist Sutras" reflects the process of Buddhism taking root from India to China, highlighting the open and inclusive culture of the Central Plains. Allusions of "Standing in the Snow to Wait upon Master Cheng" and "Xu Heng Wouldn't Eat Pears Without the Owner's Permission" depict the formation and dissemination of Neo-Confucianism advocated by Cheng Hao, Cheng Yi and Zhu Xi, the most vital school of Confucianism after the Song and Yuan dynasties.

Henan, located in the middle of China, has played a key role in political and military strategies of China. Since ancient times, there has been a saying that those who win the Central Plains win the nation. Henan witnessed major historical events that shaped China's history. King Zhuang of the State of Chu searched for the tripod in the Central Plains (attempting to usurp the throne) in the Eastern Zhou Dynasty. The classic story of "Besieging Wei to Rescue Zhao" (that is, relieving the besieged by besieging the base of the besiegers) is set in the Warring States Period. The story of the delimitation of the Chu River and Han Boundary (the borders of two opposing powers) when General Liu Bang and General Xiang Yu competed for the throne at the turn from the Qin Dynasty to the Han Dynasty tells of the border between two opposing powers. The allusion about the ambition of General Cao Cao reveals that he dreamed of continuing to be a great soldier, just as an old steed in the stable might still aspire to gallop on a long journey in the Three Kingdoms period. Other classical stories tell the tales of Empress Wu Zetian's pilgrimage to Song Mountain during the Tang Dynasty and the release of military power by wining and dining by Emperor Zhao Kuangyin, the founding father of the Northern Song Dynasty. Yet Henan saw a decline in its glory after the Southern Song Dynasty, as political and economic centers shifted away, and the number of corresponding allusions also dropped. However, the culture of the Central Plains still made a difference to the world civilization, by offering the most outstanding model of a civilian prince when Zhu Zaiyu invented twelve-tone equal temperament.

The selected historical allusions in this book demonstrate that the history and culture of the Central Plains is the main cradle and backbone of Chinese culture, while paying attention to entertainment and vividness. Hence readers can be exposed to a bird's-eye view of Chinese culture, appreciate it and take a sip of the glory of Henan culture and Chinese civilization through these classical stories.

目 录　　　　　　　　　　　　　　Contents

第一章　先秦典故　　　　　　　　　　001
　　一、周公测影　　　　　　　　　　002
　　二、问鼎中原　　　　　　　　　　010
　　三、孔老问礼　　　　　　　　　　014
　　四、围魏救赵　　　　　　　　　　020
　　五、杞人忧天　　　　　　　　　　026
　　六、愚公移山　　　　　　　　　　030

Chapter 1　Allusions in the Pre-Qin Period　　001
　　Ⅰ. Zhou Gong Measuring the Length of the Shadow　　003
　　Ⅱ. Coveting the Tripods in the Central Plains　　011
　　Ⅲ. Confucius Asking Laozi About Rites　　015
　　Ⅳ. Besieging Wei to Rescue Zhao　　021
　　Ⅴ. The Man of Qi Worrying About the Sky　　027
　　Ⅵ. Yugong Removing the Mountains　　031

第二章　秦汉魏晋南北朝典故　　　　　037
　　一、楚河汉界　　　　　　　　　　038
　　二、逐鹿中原　　　　　　　　　　044
　　三、白马驮经　　　　　　　　　　052
　　四、三顾茅庐　　　　　　　　　　058
　　五、老骥伏枥　　　　　　　　　　064

Chapter 2　Allusions in Qin, Han, Wei, Jin, and Southern and Northern Dynasties　　037
　　Ⅰ. The Boundary Between Chu and Han　　039

Ⅱ. Chasing the Deer in the Central Plains　　　　045
Ⅲ. The White Horse Carrying Buddhist Sutras　　053
Ⅳ. Three Visits to Zhuge Liang's Thatched Cottage　059
Ⅴ. The Old Steed over the Manger　　　　　　　065

第三章　隋唐典故　　　　　　　　　　　　　　　071
　　　一、营造东都　　　　　　　　　　　　　　072
　　　二、僧救唐王　　　　　　　　　　　　　　080
　　　三、玄奘取经　　　　　　　　　　　　　　086
　　　四、封禅嵩山　　　　　　　　　　　　　　096
　　　五、洛阳牡丹甲天下　　　　　　　　　　　102

Chapter 3　Allusions in Sui and Tang Dynasties　　071
　　　Ⅰ. Building the Eastern Capital　　　　　　073
　　　Ⅱ. Shaolin Monks Rescuing the King of Tang　081
　　　Ⅲ. Xuanzang Going to the West for the Buddhist Sutras　087
　　　Ⅳ. Feng and Shan: Offering Sacrifices on Mount Song　097
　　　Ⅴ. The Peony in Luoyang is Second to None　103

第四章　宋元明清典故　　　　　　　　　　　　　109
　　　一、杯酒释兵权　　　　　　　　　　　　　110
　　　二、程门立雪　　　　　　　　　　　　　　116
　　　三、精忠报国　　　　　　　　　　　　　　122
　　　四、许衡不食无主之梨　　　　　　　　　　128
　　　五、高风让国（朱载堉）　　　　　　　　　134
　　　六、万金济黉（康百万）　　　　　　　　　140

Chapter 4　Allusions in Song, Yuan, Ming and Qing Dynasties　　109
　　Ⅰ. Releasing the Military Power by Wining and Dining　　111
　　Ⅱ. Standing in the Snow to Wait upon Master Cheng　　117
　　Ⅲ. Serving the Country Faithfully　　123
　　Ⅳ. Xu Heng Wouldn't Eat Pears Without the Owner's Permission　　129
　　Ⅴ. Renouncing the Title of Prince (Zhu Zaiyu)　　135
　　Ⅵ. Granting Ten Thousand in Gold to Build Schools (The Millionaire Kang Family)　　141

附录：中国历史年代简表　　146
Appendix: A Brief Chronology of Chinese History　　146

第一章

先秦典故

Chapter 1

Allusions in the Pre-Qin Period

先秦时期是指公元前221年大一统的秦朝建立之前的历史时期，主要包括夏、商、西周、春秋和战国等时期。从公元前2070年中国第一个世袭制朝代——夏朝的建立算起，先秦时期有1800多年的历史。河南是中华文明重要的发源地，夏朝的国都位于河南偃师二里头，郑州、安阳是商代的都城，中原地区更是春秋战国时期兵家必争之地，各种思想流派在此孕育、交流、发展。

一、周公测影

"宅兹中国"（居住于位于天下中央的王国），是华夏先民们孜孜以求的美好愿望。"中央王国"观念的产生，与中国古人对大地的认识息息相关。中国古人认为大地是平的，大小是有限的。如此一来，大地的表面必然就会有一个中心。那么，大地的中心在哪里呢？大地的中心就在今天河南省登封市告成镇，古代称为阳城，此处也是世界文化遗产"天地之中"所在地。阳城被认为是"天地之中"，则源于周公测影的典故。

尧、舜、禹是中国人心目中远古时代最圣明的三位帝王。他们三位没有基于血缘关系进行王位继承，而是将王位传给德才兼备的贤者。尧去世后，王位传给了舜。舜打算将王位传给禹，但禹非常谦让，坚持舜应该把王位传给舜的儿子。舜死后，禹因此迁徙到阳城居住。天下的百姓追随禹来到了阳城，而不是尊奉舜的儿子为他们的国君。阳城也就成为中国第一个王朝——夏朝的国都，但阳城被认为是大地的中心，则要到周朝时期。

夏朝之后是商朝，商朝最后一位国君殷纣王荒淫无道。居住在陕西一带的诸侯周武王推翻了商朝，建立了周朝。周武王死后，他的儿子成王继位。但是成王年幼，只能由周武王的弟弟周公来辅佐成王处理朝政。

The Pre-Qin period refers to the historical period before the establishment of the unified Qin Dynasty in 221 BC, mainly consisting of the Xia Dynasty, the Shang Dynasty, the Western Zhou Dynasty, the Spring and Autumn Period and the Warring States Period. The Pre-Qin period lasted for more than 1800 years since the establishment of the Xia Dynasty—the first hereditary dynasty in China in 2070 BC. Henan is the important birthplace of Chinese civilization. The state capital of the Xia Dynasty was located in Erlitou, Yanshi City of Henan Province, while Zhengzhou and Anyang were the capital cities of the Shang Dynasty. The Central Plains region was also a place of contention for strategists in the Spring and Autumn and Warring States periods. Various schools of thought were bred, exchanged and developed here.

I. Zhou Gong Measuring the Length of the Shadow

"Dwelling in Zhongguo" (living in the kingdom in the middle of the world) is a good wish assiduously pursued by Chinese ancestors. The concept of "the Middle Kingdom" is closely related to the ancient Chinese' understanding of the earth. The ancient Chinese believed that the earth was flat and its size was limited, and hence there must be a center on the surface of the earth. But where is the center of the earth? It is located precisely in Gaocheng Town, Dengfeng City, Henan Province today, at a site which was called Yangcheng in ancient times. It is also the seat of the world cultural heritage—"The Center of Heaven and Earth". Yangcheng derives its status as "The Center of Heaven and Earth" from the story of Zhou Gong (the Duke of Zhou) measuring the length of the shadow cast by the sun.

Yao, Shun and Yu are the three most intelligent and enlightened emperors in ancient times in the eyes of Chinese people. Instead of passing down and succeeding to the throne based on the blood relationship, they passed the throne to a sage with both ability and virtue. When Yao died, the throne was passed to Shun. Shun intended to pass the throne to Yu, but Yu was very humble and insisted that Shun should pass the throne to his own son. So after Shun died, Yu moved to Yangcheng. However, all the people went to Yangcheng seeking Yu, refusing to take Shun's son as their king. Therefore, Yangcheng became the capital

当时周朝偏居西方,治理统一后的国家多有不便。为了更好地惩恶扬善、治理国家,便于政令的下达和赋税的征收,周公决定在地中附近建立都城以治理天下。

为了找出大地的中心,周公采用了立表测影的方法。中国古代的儒家经典著作《周礼》中明确规定,在夏至日,立八尺长的表,测量表的影长如果为一尺五寸,则立表处即为地中。周公采用这个方法进行测量,最终确定大地的中心是阳城。

至此,阳城与儒家文化中两位最重要的贤者大禹和周公联系了起来。

周公测景台

Zhou Gong's Observation Tower

of the Xia Dynasty, the first dynasty in China. But it was not until the Zhou Dynasty that Yangcheng was regarded as the center of the earth.

The Xia Dynasty was followed by the Shang Dynasty. King Zhou, the last ruler of the Shang Dynasty, was extremely profligate and licentious. King Wu of Zhou, a vassal living in Shaanxi, overthrew the Shang Dynasty and established the Zhou Dynasty. After the death of King Wu of Zhou, his son succeeded to the throne, and became known as King Cheng. However, King Cheng, too young to handle the affairs of the state, had to be assisted by Zhou Gong (the Duke of Zhou), the younger brother of King Wu of Zhou. At that time, it was a hard task to govern the unified country because the capital of the Zhou Dynasty was located in the far west of the country. In order to better punish the evil and promote the good, govern the country, and facilitate the issuance of government decrees and the collection of taxes, Zhou Gong decided to establish the capital near the center of the earth.

To find out the center of the earth, Zhou Gong adopted the method of erecting a measuring stick on the ground to measure the length of the shadow cast by the sun. In *The Rites of Zhou*, an ancient Confucian classic in China, it is clearly stipulated that on the summer solstice, an 8-chi-long (about 184.8 centimeters) rod should be erected serving as a measuring stick. By calculation, if the shadow cast of the measuring stick is 1.5 *chis* (about 30 centimeters) long, the place where the measuring stick is erected is the center of the earth. With this method, Zhou Gong finally determined that Yangcheng was the center of the earth.

Yangcheng was linked with two most important sages in Confucian culture—Yu and Zhou Gong. As the capital city during Yu's reign, Yangcheng acquired special political significance because it was the place both where the state capital was located and where the popular will inclined at the same time. On the other hand, with Zhou Gong measuring the length of the shadow cast by the sun, Yangcheng was determined to be the center of the earth. Since then, the notion of Yangcheng as the center of the earth has been widespread and recognized by people. In light of the great achievement of Zhou Gong's shadow measurement and the unique position of the notion of Yangcheng as the center of the earth in astronomy, the ancients regarded Yangcheng as the best place for astronomical

禹都阳城，因使阳城与国都所在和民心所向联系起来而具备了特殊的政治含义。周公测影，则通过测量认定大地的中心在阳城。此后，阳城为地中的观念广泛传播开来，得到人们的普遍认可。鉴于周公测影的伟业和阳城地中说在天文学上独一无二的地位，古人把它视为天文观测的最佳场所。自西周以后，历代许多天文学家都专程在此地进行天文观测，留下了一些历史古迹。

今天我们在登封看到的周公测景台，通高 3.91 米，下部是上小下大的方形石座，称作"圭"，上部为长方形石柱，称作"表"。据说圭和表当初都是木制的，开元年间，唐玄宗命太史监南宫说仿照周公土圭旧制，换成石圭、石表，现石表上刻有"周公测景臺"楷书字样。这个测景台，并不具备实用性，只是为了纪念周公测量地中的行为。若从周公测量日影算起，测景台至今已有 3000 多年的历史。

测景台后面，可看见一砖石结构的建筑，这就是元代天文学家郭守敬创建的观星台。据说元世祖忽必烈统一中国后，任用著名天文学家郭守敬等进行历法改革。郭守敬在全国各地设立了 27 个观测站，而观测的中心设在哪里呢？郭守敬犯了愁，接连几天茶饭不思，害了一场大病。有一天，突然来了一位长者，声言能给他看病，未经把脉就递上一张药方。郭守敬接过一看，只见上面写着：天心一个，地胆一枚，中药滋阳。正待询问，长者已不知去向。郭守敬反复思量，便恍然大悟，连说"此药妙矣！"，其他人有些不解，问这些药到哪里去找。郭守敬答道，此药方写得很明白，中药滋阳就是中岳之阳，所谓天心、地胆就在嵩山。郭守敬火速赶到嵩山脚下，下马一问，连七岁小儿也能对答：天有心，地有胆，天心地胆阳城镇。郭守敬便在此建起了中心观星台。登封的这

observation. Since the period of the Western Zhou Dynasty, astronomers of all dynasties have gone to Yangcheng for astronomical observation, leaving behind some historical relics.

Today people can come to Dengfeng for a visit to Zhou Gong's Observation Tower. The tower stands 3.91 meters high. The lower part of the tower is a square stone pedestal called "Gui" with a small upper part and a large lower part, and the upper part of the tower being a rectangular stone pillar, is called "Biao". It is said that both "Gui" and "Biao" were originally made of wood. During the Kaiyuan reign period (a flourishing period in the Tang Dynasty), Emperor Xuanzong of the Tang Dynasty ordered Nangong Yue, assistant director of astrology, to make "Gui" and "Biao" out of stone following the form of Zhou Gong's "Tu Gui" (earth sundial). Now the "Biao" made of stone (in Dengfeng) is engraved with the characters "周公测景臺"(Zhou Gong's Observation Tower). This tower is built to commemorate Zhou Gong's contribution to determining the center of the earth by measuring the length of the shadow cast by the sun and is not to be used for real measuring. From the time when Zhou Gong measured the length of the shadow to determine the center of the earth, this tower has a history of more than 3000 years.

Behind the Observation Tower is a brick and stone structure. This is the Astronomical Observatory built by Guo Shoujing, an astronomer of the Yuan Dynasty. The story goes that after Kublai Khan, known as the Shizu of the Yuan Dynasty, unified China, he appointed the famous astronomer Guo Shoujing to carry out a calendar reform. For this purpose, Guo Shoujing set up 27 observation stations all over the country with the location of the observation center remaining undetermined. Guo Shoujing thought about the issue from dawn to dusk. He was so worried that for several days he lost his appetite for food and drink and even fell ill. One day, an old man paid Guo Shoujing a visit claiming that he could cure Guo Shoujing. Without feeling Guo Shoujing's pulse for diagnosis, the mysterious old man handed him a prescription. Guo Shoujing found it said: one heavenly heart, one earthly gall, and nourishing Yang with Chinese medicine. Feeling puzzled, Guo Shoujing was going to inquire more only to find the old man had disappeared. Thinking it over and over again, Guo Shoujing finally got at the implied information. "What a wonderful prescription!" he exclaimed. All the

座观星台，就是当时全国的中心观测站，也是唯一一处保存至今的观测站点。

测量地中是中国古人地平大地观的产物，周公测影的行为则使地中观念有了更加深厚的文化内涵。如今保存在河南登封的周公测景台和登封观星台，成为中国传统"地中"观念的实物见证。从古人的观念看来，此处也是"中国"的标志所在。

others were still at a loss and they asked him where to find these medicines. Guo Shoujing replied that everything was clearly stated in the prescription. Nourishing Yang with traditional Chinese medicine (Zhong Yao Zi Yang) refers to Yang of the Central Mountain (Zhong Yue Zhi Yang). So the so-called heavenly heart and earthly gall should be found in the Central Mountain (Zhong Yue)—Mount Song. Guo Shoujing hurried to the foot of Mount Song and found that even a seven-year-old child there knew that the heaven has the heart, and the earth has the gall, and that both are to be found in Yangcheng town. Therefore, Guo Shoujing built a central observatory there. The observatory in Dengfeng is not only the central observatory in China at that time, but also remains the only one preserved to this day.

Zhou Gong's determination of the center of the earth by measuring the length of the shadow originates from the Chinese ancients' view that the earth is flat and reveals a profound cultural origin of the notion that there is a center on the earth. Both Zhou Gong's Observation Tower and the Astronomical Observatory in Dengfeng, Henan Province bear witness to the traditional Chinese concept of "the center of the earth". From the view of the ancients, these two places are also the emblems of "Zhongguo" (the Middle Kingdom) .

二、问鼎中原

传说古代夏禹铸造九鼎,代表九州,作为国家权力的象征。夏、商、周三代以九鼎为传国重器,为得天下者所据有。周朝分为西周(公元前1046年—前771年)和东周(公元前770年—前256年)两个时期。周朝由周武王姬发创建,定都镐京(今陕西西安)。周成王时营建成周(今河南洛阳),并在此举行祭祀、赏赐臣子的一系列活动。公元前771年,镐京陷落,西周灭亡。公元前770年(周平王元年),平王东迁,定都

问鼎中原
Coveting the Tripods in the Central Plains

II. Coveting the Tripods in the Central Plains

The legend has it that Yu of the Xia Dynasty forged nine tripods as a symbol of the state power, representing the 9 administrative regions in ancient China. In the Xia, Shang and Zhou dynasties, the nine tripods were passed on as national treasures, playing an important role in passing the throne to the next ruler and transferring power to those who were in the position to rule the country. The Zhou Dynasty was divided into two periods: the Western Zhou Dynasty (1046 BC-771 BC) and the Eastern Zhou Dynasty (770 BC -256 BC). The Zhou Dynasty was founded by Ji Fa, King Wu of the Zhou Dynasty, with Haojing (now Xi'an, Shaanxi) as the capital. King Cheng of the Zhou Dynasty constructed and developed Chengzhou (now Luoyang, Henan) where a series of activities were held to offer sacrifices and reward officials. In 771 BC, Haojing fell and the Western Zhou Dynasty perished. In 770 BC (the first year of the reign of King Ping of Zhou), King Ping moved eastward and chose Chengzhou as the capital, hence starting the period of the Eastern Zhou Dynasty. The Western Zhou Dynasty and the Eastern Zhou Dynasty are collectively referred to as the Zhou Dynasty in history books. With "the division of Jin by three rival families" as the watershed, the Eastern Zhou Dynasty was further divided into the Spring and Autumn Period and the Warring States Period.

At the end of the Spring and Autumn Period, many feudal lords vied for the throne as the power of the royal family of the Zhou Dynasty declined. According to *Commentary on the "Spring and Autumn Annals"*, in 606 BC, King Zhuang of the Chu State, after defeating the Rong ethic group in Luhun, arrived at Luoyang, the capital city of Zhou. King Ding of Zhou sent Wang Sunman to receive and reward the king of Chu and to inquire about his real intention. During the talk, King Zhuang of Chu was conceited enough to ask Wang Sunman about the size and weight of the nine tripods of the Zhou royal family. It was evident that King Zhuang of Chu blatantly coveted the throne. At that time, the royal family of Zhou was too weak to deter King Zhuang of Chu, but Wang Sunman answered with due dignity: "What is most important is the ruler's virtue instead of a tripod. Yu of the Xia Dynasty won the support of all the vassals because he had virtue.

成周，此后周朝的这段时期称为东周。史书又将西周和东周合称为两周。其中东周以"三家分晋"为节点，又分为春秋和战国两个时期。

春秋末年，周室衰微，群雄争霸，据《左传》记载，公元前606年楚庄王伐陆浑之戎，兵至洛阳。周定王派王孙满犒劳楚庄王，顺便打听楚庄王虚实。两人相谈之间，楚庄王竟问王孙满周王室九鼎的大小轻重。楚庄王觊觎王位之心已然毫不遮掩，周王室虽然权势衰微奈何不得，但王孙满却用不卑不亢的回答替周天子挽回了颜面。王孙满说："在德不在鼎。当初夏禹是因为有德，天下诸侯都拥戴他，各地才贡献铜材，启才能铸成九鼎以象万物。后来夏桀昏乱，鼎就转移给了商；商纣暴虐，鼎又转移给了周。如果天子有德，鼎虽小却重得难以转移；如果天子无德，鼎虽大却是轻而易动。周朝的国运还未完，鼎的轻重是不可以问的。"楚庄王自然也明白此时尚有晋、齐、吴等诸侯大国在，局势条件远不足以称霸天下，便退兵了。

夏朝经历了470年，到公元前1600年，夏桀无道亡国，九鼎为成汤所得，成汤就建立了商朝。商朝经历550多年，到公元前1046年，纣王暴虐亡国，九鼎为姬发所得，姬发就建立了周朝。到公元前606年之时，周王室衰微已久，此时实力渐渐强大的楚庄王想取周而代之，就借朝拜天子的名义，到周王室去问九鼎的大小轻重，结果王孙满高超的外交辞令着实让楚庄王碰了一鼻子灰，这个话题也就没再继续下去。但从此以后，人们习惯用"问鼎"指代夺取政权。

For this reason, people of all regions contributed copper materials so that Qi of the Xia Dynasty was able to cast the nine tripods representing all the things in the world. Later, as Jie of the Xia Dynasty was a fatuous ruler, the tripods were transferred to the Shang Dynasty. King Zhou of Shang was tyrannical, so the tripods were transferred to the Zhou Dynasty. If the ruler has virtue, the tripods would be too heavy to be moved and transferred no matter how small they are; conversely, if the ruler has no virtue, the tripods would become light and easy to be moved no matter how large they are. Since the royal family of Zhou is still in power and the reign of the Zhou Dynasty will continue, it is inappropriate to ask about the weight of the tripods at present." Hearing these words, King Zhuang of Chu knew it was still not the right time for him to seize the throne and become the ruler as there were still such great vassal states as Jin, Qi, and Wu. So he withdrew his troops.

The Xia Dynasty lasted 470 years. In 1600 BC, Xia perished as a result of the fatuousness and self-indulgence of Jie of Xia. The nine tripods were obtained by Chengtang, who established the Shang Dynasty. The Shang Dynasty lasted more than 550 years until 1046 BC when the state was demolished as a result of King Zhou's tyranny and the nine tripods were obtained by Ji Fa, who established the Zhou Dynasty. By 606 BC, as the power of the royal family of Zhou had been declining for a long time, the powerful King Zhuang of Chu wanted to usurp the throne. So he went to ask the Zhou royal family about the size and weight of the nine tripods in the name of worshiping the king of Zhou, the ruler of the country. But with Wang Sunman's ingenious diplomatic language, King Zhuang of Chu was snubbed and dropped the topic. But from then on, "coveting the tripods" has been used to mean "usurping the throne".

三、孔老问礼

孔子,名丘,字仲尼,鲁国陬邑(今山东省曲阜市)人,祖籍宋国栗邑(今河南省夏邑县),出身贵族之家,博学多闻,年轻时就有报国救世的理想,积极从事政治活动和聚徒讲学,50岁后曾在鲁国做官,是中国古代著名的思想家、政治家、教育家,儒家学派创始人。老子,姓李名耳,字聃,一字伯阳,或曰谥伯阳,春秋末期人,生卒年不详,籍贯也多有争议,《史记》记载老子出生于陈国,中国古代思想家、哲学家、文学家和史学家,道家学派创始人和主要代表人物,与庄子并称"老庄"。

公元前523年的一天,孔子对弟子南宫敬叔说:"周之守藏室史老聃,博古通今,知礼乐之源,明道德之要。今吾欲去周求教,汝愿同去否?"南宫敬叔欣然同意,随即请示当时鲁国的国君。鲁国国君批准后,派遣一辆二马拉的马车、一个书童、一个车夫,由南宫敬叔陪孔子前往东周。

老子见孔子千里迢迢而来,非常高兴,彻夜长谈之后,带孔子访大夫苌弘。苌弘善乐,授孔子乐律、乐理;引孔子观看祭神之典,考查周国的教育基地和祭祀礼仪,使孔子感叹不已,获益匪浅。在周国待了数日,孔子向老子辞行。老子送孔子到当时的驿馆之外,就说:"吾闻之,富贵者送人以财,仁义者送人以言。吾不富不贵,无财以送汝,愿以数言相送。当今之世,聪明而深察者,其所以遇难而几至于死,在于好讥人之非也;善辩而通达者,其所以招祸而屡至于身,在于好扬人之恶也。为人之子,勿以己为高;为人之臣,勿以己为上,望汝切记。"孔子顿首道:"弟子一定谨记在心!"

回到鲁国,众弟子问道:"先生拜访老子,是否见到老子本尊了呢?"孔子道:"当然见到了。"弟子问。"老子是怎样的人呢?"孔子道:"鸟,我知它能飞;鱼,我知它能游;兽,我知它能跑。跑

III. Confucius Asking Laozi About Rites

Confucius, whose original name is Kong Qiu, literary name is Zhongni, and ancestral home is Liyi (now Xiayi County, Henan Province) of the State of Song, was born in Zouyi (now Qufu City, Shandong Province) of the State of Lu. Born and bred in a noble family, Confucius was erudite and aspired to serve the country and save the world when he was young. So he actively engaged himself in political activities and gave lectures to his disciples. In his fifties, he became an official in the State of Lu. Confucius was a renowned thinker, politician, educator and the founder of Confucianism in ancient China. Laozi, whose family name is Li, given name is Er and literary name is Dan or Boyang (Boyang may be his posthumous name according to some records), was born and lived in the late Spring and Autumn Period. The years of his birth and death are unknown and his native place is also controversial. According to *Shiji* (*Records of the Grand Historian*), Laozi was born in the State of Chen. He was an ancient Chinese thinker, philosopher, writer and historian, the founder and main representative of Daoism. Laozi and Zhuangzi (another representative of Daoism) became known as "Lao Zhuang".

One day in 523 BC, Confucius said to his disciple Nangong Jingshu, "Lao Dan, curator of the royal archives at the court of the Zhou Dynasty, is erudite and well-informed. He knows the origin of rites and music, and understands the essence of morality. Now I want to go to Zhou to learn from him. Would you like to go with me?" Nangong Jingshu readily agreed and immediately asked for permission from the king of Lu. With the king's approval, Confucius and Nangong Jingshu set off to Eastern Zhou in a carriage and pair accompanied by an attendant and a coachman.

Laozi was delighted to see Confucius coming all the way to visit him and he talked with Confucius for the whole night. The next day, Laozi took Confucius to visit a senior official named Chang Hong who was good at music and Changhong taught Confucius musical temperament and theories. Then Confucius watched the ceremony of offering sacrifices to gods, visited the educational base, and studied the sacrificial rites of the State of Zhou, which impressed him deeply and benefited him a lot. After several days' stay in the State of Zhou, Confucius bade

者可用网缚之，游者可用钩钓之，飞者可用箭取之。至于龙，我却不知道怎么抓住它。龙乘风云而上九天也！我所见到的老子，大概就是龙吧！学识渊深而莫测，志趣高邈而难知；如蛇之随时屈伸，如龙之应时变化。老聃，真吾师也！"

孔老问礼
Confucius Asking Laozi About Rites

以上故事主要来自《史记》中所记载的孔老问礼。其实在先秦典籍中，道家学派的《庄子》、儒家学派的《礼记》和综合各家学派的《吕氏春秋》，都不约而同地记载了"孔子问礼于老子"这件事，只不过各自记载的故事侧重点有所不同。此外，汉代的《韩诗外传》也记载了"孔

farewell to Laozi. Escorting Confucius outside the posthouse where he stayed, Laozi said, "It is said that the rich give money to others, while the righteous give words to others. Since I am not rich, I have no money to give you. But I am willing to give you a few words. In today's world, the wise men who can keenly perceive the problems may get into trouble and even die because they tend to deride the wrongs of others; the eloquent men who have a deep and thorough understanding of the world may invite disasters to themselves because they tend to publicize the evils of others. Therefore, be always reverent to your elders and modest to your superiors. I hope you will remember my words." Confucius replied with a nod, "I will keep them in mind!"

Back to the State of Lu, the disciples asked Confucius, "Did you see Laozi in person?" Confucius said, "Of course I did." "What is he like?" asked the disciples. Confucius said: "A bird, I know it can fly; a fish, I know it can swim; a beast, I know it can run. To catch those that can run, we can use nets; to catch those that can swim, we can use hooks; and to get those that can fly, we can use arrows. But when it comes to a dragon, I don't know how to catch it as I cannot understand how it ascends into the sky riding the wind and the clouds. Laozi is just like a dragon! His knowledge is profound and immeasurable, and his aspiration is high and unfathomable. He can be as flexible as a snake and as adaptable as a dragon with the change of the situation. Lao Dan is indeed my true teacher!"

The above story is taken from the record of Confucius asking Laozi about rites in *Shiji*. In fact, the meeting between Confucius and Laozi is recorded in many classics of the Pre-Qin period including *Zhuangzi* of the Daoist school, the *Book of Rites* of the Confucian school, and the *Spring and Autumn Annals of Master Lv* containing thoughts of various schools. But different versions of the story focus on different aspects. In addition, the same story, in *Han Shi Wai Zhuan (Outer Commentary on the Book of Songs by Master Han)* of the Han Dynasty, is recorded under the title "Confucius Learning from Lao Dan", while in the *Confucius Family Language*, it is called "Confucius Inquiring of Laozi About Dao (the natural order of the universe)". Additionally, a large number of unearthed stone reliefs of the Han Dynasty portraying "Confucius Visiting Laozi" show that people of the Han Dynasty firmly believed that Confucius did visit Laozi and learn from him.

子学于老聃",《孔子家语》也有"孔子问道于老子"的记载,且大量出土的汉代"孔子见老子"画像石表明,汉代民众心中笃信孔子确实向老子问礼学习过。

  孔子在众弟子心中已然是能够"博学于文,约之以礼"的真君子,但孔子却相当谦虚好学,一生都在认真追求学问的新境界。不论是对方是黄口小儿,还是如老子这般跟自己学问、政见不同的学者,他都虚心求教。孔老问礼的故事,不论真假,都能够激励后世儒生砥砺学问,不失为一桩美谈。

In the minds of all his disciples, Confucius was already a man of noble character who could "restrain himself and abide by rites while learning widely", but he remained modest and eager to learn in all his life, constantly striving to transcend himself in the realm of knowledge. Be it a naïve and ignorant child or a scholar like Laozi with intellectual and political views disparate from his own, he was always ready to listen to their advice. True or fictitious, the story of Confucius asking Laozi about rites is definitely instructive and enlightening, inspiring later Confucian scholars to sharpen their knowledge.

四、围魏救赵

战国时，魏国围攻赵国都城邯郸，赵国求救于齐国。齐将田忌、孙膑率军救赵，趁魏国都城兵力空虚，引兵直攻魏国。魏军回救，齐军乘其疲惫，于中途大败魏军，遂解赵围。（事见《史记·孙子吴起列传》）这个典故是指采用包抄敌人的后方来迫使敌人撤兵的战术，源自大军事家孙膑。孙膑原本与庞涓一起学习兵法，庞涓出师后选择辅佐魏国，但他知道自己不如孙膑有才，因此想了一条毒计。庞涓把孙膑诱骗到魏国，

围魏救赵
Besieging Wei to Rescue Zhao

Ⅳ. Besieging Wei to Rescue Zhao

During the Warring States Period (in 353 BC), the State of Wei besieged Handan, the capital of the State of Zhao. So, the State of Zhao asked for assistance from the State of Qi. Two generals of Qi, Tian Ji and Sun Bin, were sent to rescue Zhao. Since the army of Wei had been dispatched to besiege Handan, the capital of Wei was poorly guarded. The two generals of Qi led their troops to attack Wei directly. As a result, the Wei army had to hurry back home for rescue. Knowing that all the soldiers of Wei were exhausted, the Qi army attacked the Wei army midway in their retreat and smashed them, relieving Zhao of the siege (recorded in "Biographies of Sun Zi and Wu Qi" in *Shiji*). This allusion refers to the tactic initiated by Sun Bin, the great military strategist in ancient China and known as besieging the base of the besieger to force him to withdraw his troops. Previously, Sun Bin and Pang Juan had both been disciples studying military strategies under the same master. Upon graduation, Pang Juan chose to serve the State of Wei. Knowing that he was not so talented as Sun Bin, and fearing Sun Bin would surpass him, he made a wicked scheme against Sun Bin. He lured Sun Bin to the State of Wei, cut off his feet, and tattooed his face, trying to destroy Sun Bin completely. Fortunately, when an envoy of the State of Qi went to Daliang (the capital of the State of Wei), he found that Sun Bin was no ordinary person, so he secretly brought Sun Bin back to the State of Qi. It was only then that Sun Bin had the opportunity to display his military talents.

In the third year of the reign of King Wei of Qi (354 BC), King Hui of Wei, unable to let go of the fact that he had yielded Zhongshan (a small country adjacent to Wei during the Eastern Zhou Dynasty and conquered by Wei for many years) to the State of Zhao, sent a great general named Pang Juan to take it back. Pang Juan thought that it would be better to directly attack Handan, the capital of Zhao, as Zhongshan was only a tiny piece of land and close to Zhao. In this way, they could kill two birds with one stone—Zhongshan could be taken back and Zhao could be weakened. Taking Pang Juan's advice, King Hui of Wei sent 500 chariots, led by Pang Juan, to attack the State of Zhao. Under Pang Juan's skillful management and leadership, the army of Wei invincibly won

断其双脚并在他脸上刺字，要彻底毁掉孙膑。幸好齐国使者来大梁（魏国首都）的时候，看出孙膑异于常人，就偷偷将孙膑带回齐国。孙膑这才有施展自己的军事才能的机会。

齐威王三年（公元前354年），魏惠王想一泄失去中山的仇恨，便派大将庞涓前去攻打。魏将庞涓认为中山不过弹丸之地，距离赵国又很近，不如直接攻打赵国的都城邯郸，既能解旧恨又能削弱赵国，可谓一举两得。于是，魏惠王调拨五百战车，由庞涓率领，直奔赵国。庞涓治军有方，军队战无不胜，很快便包围了赵国的都城邯郸，赵国形势危急。第二年，赵国迫于无奈只得向齐国求救。齐威王任命田忌做主将，孙膑做军师，领兵前往救援。

攻击方向选在哪里呢？起初，田忌准备直奔邯郸。孙膑认为，要解开纷乱的丝线，不能用手强拉硬扯，要解决别人打架的问题，不能直接派兵解围，要避实就虚，击中要害。孙膑遂建议说："如今魏赵两国相互攻打，魏国的精锐部队必定在国外精疲力竭，老弱残兵在国内疲惫不堪。你不如率领军队火速向魏国的国都大梁挺进，占据它的交通要道，冲击它军备空虚的地方，魏国国都被围困，魏王肯定会下令庞涓放弃攻打赵国而回国自救。我们再在庞涓回师的必经之路伏击他，必定可以大获全胜。这样，我们不但可以一举解赵国之围，而且可坐收魏国自行挫败的成果。"田忌听取了孙膑的意见，出兵围困魏国的都城大梁，魏王果然下令庞涓回军自救。庞涓收到魏王的命令后，丢掉粮草辎重，星夜从赵国撤军回国。孙膑预先在魏军回国的必经之地桂陵设下埋伏。当魏军经过时，齐军突然出击，大败魏军。齐国军队大胜，赵国的危机也相应解除了。

孙膑用围攻魏国的办法来解除赵国的危困，这在我国历史上是一个很有名的战例，被后来的军事家们列为三十六计中的重要一计。围魏救赵这一避实就虚的战法为历代军事家所欣赏，至今仍有其生命力。

两点之间线段最短，这样的定理在科学研究领域是成立的，但它并

one battle after another and soon besieged Handan, the capital of Zhao. The State of Zhao was in a critical situation. The next year, the State of Zhao had no choice but to request assistance from the State of Qi. In response, King Wei of Qi sent troops to the rescue with Tian Ji as the chief general and Sun Bin as the military advisor.

But where to attack? At first, Tian Ji intended to go straight to Handan. But Sun Bin believed that to untie the tangled threads, it wouldn't work to pull them apart with great force. In the same way, to resolve a conflict between two states, it was not a good strategy to get involved in the fight. Instead, it was wise to stay clear of the enemy's main force and strike at his weakest point and hit him once and for all. Sun Bin then suggested: "Now that Wei and Zhao are deeply engaged in the war, the elite troops of Wei fighting away from home must be exhausted, and the old and weak soldiers at home must be worn out. It is my suggestion that you lead the army to rush forward to Daliang, the capital of Wei, take its traffic arteries, and attack the insufficiently guarded places of Wei. Once the State of Wei is besieged, the king of Wei will certainly command Pang Juan to stop attacking Zhao and return home to defend their capital. If we ambush Pang Juan's troops on their return journey, we can gain a complete victory. In this way, the State of Zhao can be delivered from the conflict and the State of Wei can be defeated without too much effort." Tian Ji took Sun Bin's advice and sent troops to besiege Daliang, the capital of the State of Wei. As expected, the king of Wei ordered Pang Juan to withdraw the troops and return home. Receiving the command, without a minute's delay, Pang Juan abandoned the food supplies and baggage and withdrew from Zhao on that very night, heading home. Sun Bin laid an ambush in Guiling, a stop-off the Wei army had to pass through on their way back home. When the Wei army passed by, the Qi army made a sudden attack and defeated the Wei soldiers. The Qi army won a great victory, and the crisis of Zhao was also lifted.

Sun Bin delivered the State of Zhao from trouble by besieging the State of Wei. This is a very famous battle in Chinese history and Sun Bin's tactic is listed as one of the thirty-six stratagems by later military strategists. By besieging Wei to rescue Zhao, the army avoided confronting the enemy directly and attacked its weak point instead. This tactic has been advocated by military strategists of all dynasties and is still actively used today.

不一定适用于现实生活中。当我们身陷困境时,与对手发生正面的冲突来解决问题,固然是一种方法,不过绝不是最聪明的方法。围魏救赵是三十六计中相当精彩的一种智谋,它的精彩之处在于以逆向思维的方式,以表面看来舍近求远的方法,绕开问题的表面现象,从事物的本源上去解决问题,从而取得一招制胜的神奇效果。

The theorem that a straight line is the shortest distance between two points is valid in the field of scientific research, but it does not necessarily apply to our real life. When we are in trouble, we often face the choice to solve the problem by confronting our opponents directly, but it is by no means always the smartest solution. As one of the thirty-six stratagems, besieging Wei to rescue Zhao is brilliant because of the reverse thinking it contains. Adopting this strategy, we are seemingly rejecting what is near at hand and seeking what is far away, but in fact we can see through the surface, and get to the root of the problem so as to win miraculously with only one move.

五、杞人忧天

浩瀚的宇宙蕴藏着无数的谜团，吸引着人类孜孜以求地去探索、破解。中国古人也一直在探索宇宙和天空的奥秘，杞人忧天是其中非常具有代表性的故事，这个故事就发生在河南省开封市杞县。

杞人忧天
The Man of Qi Worrying About the Sky

相传，古代杞国有个人，他整天担忧天会崩塌下来，地会塌陷下去，自己无处安身。因为害怕发生这种情况，他白天吃不下饭，夜里不敢睡觉。杞人的朋友看到他每天因为害怕天地崩坠而忧愁烦闷的样子，就去劝解他说："天，就是一股积聚的气体，到处都是气。人的一举一动、一呼一吸都要和它接触。你整天在气体里活动，为什么还要担心它会塌下来呢？"

这个杞人反问道："如果天真的是一股积聚的气体，那么太阳、月亮和星星不就掉下来了吗？"杞人的朋友回答："太阳、月亮、星星也不过是气体中会发光的物质，它们不会掉下来。就算是掉下来，也不会伤到人的。"杞人又问："那么地要是塌下去怎么办呢？"那人回答道："地不过是堆积起来的土块罢了。东西南北到处都有这样的土块，没有地方是没有土块的。你走路、跑步、蹦跳，不是成天都在地上活动吗？为什么会担心它会塌陷下去呢？"杞人听了，消除了疑虑，一解愁容，

V. The Man of Qi Worrying About the Sky

Human beings, enchanted by the countless mysteries in the vast universe, have been exploring the universe relentlessly to solve them. Chinese ancients also wondered about and delved into the mysteries of the universe and the sky. Among these ancients is a man who worried that the sky might fall. The story about this man is set in Qi County, Kaifeng City of Henan Province.

According to the story, a man in the ancient State of Qi worried all day long that the sky would fall down and the earth would sink, leaving him nowhere to hide. He was so much haunted by the idea that he could not eat during the day and dared not sleep at night. Trying to palliate his worry, his friend told him: "The sky is formed by the accumulation of air. There is no place where there is no air. Whenever you move or breathe, you are living right in the air. Why do you ever need to worry that the sky will fall down?"

The man rejoined, "If the sky were really nothing but air, would not the sun, the moon and the stars fall down?" To this, his friend answered, "The sun, the moon and the stars are nothing but bright things in the air. They won't fall down. Even if they should fall down, they would not hurt anybody." "But what if the earth should sink?" And the other replied, "The earth is also only formed of piled-up clods, which can be found anywhere. There is no place where there are no clods. As you walk, run and jump on the ground, you are moving the whole day on this earth. Why do you ever need to worry that it may collapse?" With this, the man's doubts were dispelled and he was gladly relieved. So was the persuader for successfully relieving his friend of his worry.

Reading this story, many would laugh at the man of Qi for his worrying about impossible things. They believe thinking about such meaningless problems is asking for trouble. In fact, behind this story lies profound astronomical thought, which reflects the desire of the man of Qi and his friend to explore the vast universe.

The man's worry about the collapse of the sky stems from his understanding of the cosmic structure or the "Gaitian Theory" (the theory of the canopy-heavens or the theory of the sky covering the earth). According to this theory, the sky

非常高兴。那位开导他的朋友，因为解除了杞人的忧愁，也十分欢喜。

许多人看到这则故事，常常会嘲笑杞人忧虑于那些根本不可能发生的事情，思考这类毫无意义的问题本身就是自寻烦恼。其实，这则故事背后蕴含了非常深刻的天文学思想，反映了杞人和他的朋友对广袤宇宙的探索之心。

杞人之所以担忧天会崩塌，源于他对宇宙结构的认识——"盖天说"。"盖天说"主张天地是两个中央凸起的平行平面，天在上，地在下，天与地之间的距离是8万里。"盖天说"天上地下的宇宙模式，为人神分离的神话提供了理想的依据。"盖天说"自身的理论缺陷在于天如何能悬空而不坠落，因为中国古人认为天是固体的，"女娲补天"的神话就是对这一观念的反映。

在"女娲补天"的神话中，当天出了问题，有了裂缝，不能完全笼罩大地时，女娲用其炼制的五色石，把天的缺口修补好。苍天有缝隙，以及这个缝隙可以用五色石填补，已经说明天是固体的。杞人同样秉持固体天壳的观念，认为天和地一样是固体，是会崩塌的，所以他才会焦虑不已，以致寝食难安。

杞人朋友的一番解释，消解了杞人的忧虑。杞人的朋友认为天纯粹由气体组成，所以便不会有天会崩塌现象的产生。杞人朋友相信的是另外一种不同的宇宙结构——"宣夜说"。"宣夜说"认为天的本质是虚空，没有一定的形体和质地。人们之所以认为天有质地，是因为天太高了、太广阔了，导致人们在观察时产生了错觉，就像人们俯瞰万丈深谷时，以为深谷是黑色的。其实深谷中是虚空，没有颜色，一切都是人类的错觉。"宣夜说"的缺陷在于，它主张天体之间相互独立，没有规律可循。"宣夜说"杜绝了人们探寻自然规律的可能性，无法给人们提供有用的信息，是一种初级的宇宙理论，因此渐渐被边缘化，被天文学家抛弃。

杞人忧天故事中所反映的宇宙结构非常朴素，现在看来甚至可能有一些可笑，可这却是人类对宇宙认识最真实的记载。它反映了人们在早期文明阶段对宇宙的好奇和探索，体现了中国古人对广袤宇宙的思考。

and the earth are two flat surfaces parallel with each other bulging in the center. The sky is above the earth with a distance of 80,000 *lis* (40,000 kilometers). The cosmological mode of the sky covering the earth advocated by "Gaitian Theory" provides an ideal basis for the myth of the separation of man and God. The problem with "Gaitian Theory" is how the sky can be suspended in the air without falling, since the ancient Chinese believed that the sky was solid, an idea reflected in the myth of "Nvwa Mending the Sky".

In the myth of "Nvwa Mending the Sky", when there was a gap in the sky, and the earth could not be completely covered, Nvwa repaired the gap with five colored stones she had tempered. The myth that there was a gap in the sky and this gap could be filled with five colored stones showed that the sky must be solid. The man of Qi held the same idea, believing the sky, being solid like the earth, could collapse. That's why he was anxious to the extent that he couldn't sleep and eat.

The man of Qi's friend's explanation dispelled his anxiety. His friend believed that the sky was made up of nothing but air and therefore could not fall down. The notion held by his friend is another theory about cosmic structure, called the "Xuanye (ubiquitous darkness) Theory". According to the "Xuanye Theory", the sky is void without shape and texture. The reason why people think that the sky has concrete texture is that the sky is too high and too broad, which leads people to have the illusion when they observe it, just like when people look down at the deep valley, they tend to think that the valley is black which in fact is void without any color. All that is but human beings' illusion. The drawback of "Xuanye Theory" is that it advocates that celestial bodies are independent of each other with no law to follow and hence rules out the possibility of exploring the laws of nature and fails to provide people with useful information. It is only a rudimentary cosmological theory and is gradually marginalized and abandoned by astronomers.

The cosmic structure embodied in the story of the man of Qi worrying about the sky is very simple and may even be absurd in the eyes of people today. But it is indeed the true record of people's understanding of the universe and reflects people's curiosity about and the exploration of the universe in the early stage of Chinese civilization, and bears witness to ancient Chinese' meditation on the vast universe.

六、愚公移山

　　太行、王屋两座山，方圆七百里，高七八千丈，本来在冀州南边、黄河北岸的北边。相传北山下面有个名叫愚公的人，年纪快到90岁了，在山的正对面居住。他苦于山区北部的阻塞，出来进去都要绕道，就召集全家人商量说："我跟你们尽力挖平险峻的大山，使道路一直通到豫州南部，到达汉水南岸，好吗？"大家纷纷表示赞同。他的妻子提出疑问说："凭你的力气，连魁父这座小山都不能削平，又能把太行、王屋怎么样呢？再说，往哪儿搁挖下来的土和石头？"众人说："把它扔到渤海的边上、隐土的北边。"于是愚公率领儿孙中能挑担子的三个人上了山，凿石头，挖土，用箕畚运到渤海边上。邻居京城氏的寡妇有个孤儿，刚七八岁，蹦蹦跳跳地去帮助他。冬夏换季，他们才能往返一次。

　　河曲的智叟讥笑愚公，阻止他干这件事，说："你简直太愚蠢了！就凭你残余的岁月，剩下的力气连山上的一棵草都动不了，又能把泥土、石头怎么样呢？"北山愚公长叹说："你的思想真顽固，顽固得没法开窍，连孤儿、寡妇都比不上。即使我死了，还有儿子在呀！儿子又生孙子，孙子又生儿子；儿子又有儿子，儿子又有孙子；子子孙孙无穷无尽，可是山却不会增高加大，还怕挖不平吗？"河曲智叟无话可答。

　　握着蛇的山神听说了，怕他没完没了地挖下去，便向天帝报告了这件事。天帝被愚公的诚心感动，命令大力神夸娥氏的两个儿子背走了那两座山，一座放在朔方的东部，一座放在雍州的南部。从那时开始，冀州南部直到汉水南岸，再也没有高山阻隔了。

Ⅵ. Yugong Removing the Mountains

The Taihang and Wangwu mountains, with a radius of 700 *lis* (about 350 kilometers) and a height of about 7,000 *zhangs* (about 23.3 kilometers), originally stood in the south of Jizhou and the north of the north bank of the Yellow River. The legend goes that an old man named Yugong (literally, "foolish old man") who was almost 90 years old, lived at the foot of the mountains, directly opposite them. As the mountains blocked traffic, he and his family had to take a detour to come and go, causing them much inconvenience. So he called the whole family together to discuss the issue. "What would you say if I suggest that we remove the mountains to make a path directly to the south of Yuzhou (in today's Henan Province) and the south bank of Hanshui River (in today's Shaanxi Province)?" asked Yugong. Everyone agreed, except for his wife, who expressed her doubt, "With your strength, you can't even flatten the small hill of Mount Kuifu, let alone the huge Taihang and Wangwu mountains. Besides, where can you deposit the earth and stones?" The others said, "We can carry the earth and stones to the shore of Bohai Sea and to the north of Yintu (a place in the legend of ancient China)." So Yugong led three of his strongest children and grandchildren who can carry loads up the mountains. They broke up stones, dug earth, and transported them to the shore of Bohai Sea with large baskets. Hearing the news, many villagers pitched in. A seven-year-old boy of the widow of the neighbor Jingcheng family also went to help them happily. It was a long journey that took the old man and his crew more than half a year to travel back and forth each time. They usually left in winter and came back in summer.

An old man named Zhisou (literally, "wise old man") lived in nearby Hequ and laughed at Yugong and persuaded him to quit. He said, "How foolish you are! At your age, old and feeble as you are, you can't even take away grass on the mountain, let alone the earth and stones." Yugong heaved a sigh and said, "You are too stubborn to be wise. Even a widow and a child know better than you. Surely I will die. But even if I die, there will still be my sons and grandsons, who will have their own sons and grandsons to keep up the work. My offspring will grow, but the mountains will not. Why is it impossible to level them?" Zhisou left without a word.

A god of the mountain, holding a snake in his hands, heard about the event.

愚公移山
Yugong Removing the Mountains

愚公移山的故事流传千年，他不畏艰难的奋斗精神感动着一代又一代中国民众。到了近现代，在毛主席的再度诠释中，愚公移山又焕发了新的精神。1945年，毛主席在中共七大作闭幕词时引用该典故，对其重新诠释，赋予其崭新的时代含义，成为中国共产党人坚忍不拔、不懈奋斗精神的写照。他详细引用了中国古代愚公移山的寓言故事之后发出号召：愚公家门前有两座山，中国人民头上也有两座大山：一座叫作帝国主义，一座叫作封建主义。只要中国共产党发扬愚公移山的精神，不断地工作，动员全国人民大众一齐起来，就会推翻这两座大山。毛主席强调我们一定要坚持下去，一定要不断地工作，我们最终也会感动上帝

He was worried that the old man and his offspring would really dig endlessly and level the two mountains, so he reported to the Lord of Heaven. Moved by Yugong's determination, the Lord of Heaven commanded two giants, the sons of Kua'e, a god with immense strength, to move the mountains elsewhere. They put one mountain in the east of Shuofang and the other in the south of Yongzhou. Ever since, there were no more mountains blocking the way between southern Jizhou and the south bank of Hanshui River.

The story of "Yugong Removing the Mountains" has been passed down for thousands of years. Yugong's spirit of fighting unswervingly despite difficulties has touched and inspired generations of Chinese people. In modern times, with Chairman Mao Zedong's reinterpretation, Yugong's story had new connotations. In 1945, Mao Zedong quoted this allusion in his closing speech at the Seventh National Congress of the Communist Party of China and gave it a new meaning in line with the times. It became a portrayal of the perseverance and unremitting struggle of the Chinese Communists. Quoting in detail the fable of "Yugong Removing the Mountains", Mao Zedong issued a call: "As there are two mountains in front of Yugong's house, there are also two mountains on the Chinese people: one is imperialism and the other is feudalism. As long as the Communist Party of China carries forward the spirit of Yugong, works persistently and mobilizes the people of the whole country to rise together, these two mountains will finally be removed." Mao Zedong stressed that we must persevere and work unceasingly, and we too, would touch God's heart. Our God is none other than the masses of the Chinese people. If they stand up and dig together with us, why can't these mountains be cleared away? This metaphor is the most profound elucidation of the spirit of Yugong. Mao Zedong injected new spiritual elements into the allusion of Yugong removing the mountains with struggle as the theme word.

In 1960, 300,000 people of Linzhou, who also lived at the foot of Taihang Mountain, commenced a herculean project that lasted for ten years. With only a hammer and a shovel in their hands, they built a 1,500-km-long Hongqiqu Canal on the cliffs of Taihang Mountain. The industrious people of Linzhou leveled 1,250 hilltops, erected 151 aqueducts, dug 211 tunnels, built 12,408 hydraulic structures, and excavated 22.25 million cubic meters of earth and rock, accomplishing a

的。这个上帝不是别人,而是全国人民大众。全国人民大众和我们一道挖这两座山,有什么挖不平呢?这个比喻,可以说是对愚公精神最深刻的阐发。毛主席为愚公移山这则寓言注入了以奋斗为主题词的精神新元素。

1960年始,同样是生活在太行山脚下的30万林州人民,苦战10个春秋,靠着一锤、一铲、两只手,在太行山悬崖峭壁上修成了全长1,500千米的红旗渠。他们削平了1,250座山头,架设了151座渡槽,开凿了211个隧洞,修建各种建筑物12,408座,挖砌土石达2,225万立方米。修成的红旗渠以浊漳河为源,渠首在山西省平顺县。总干渠墙高4.3米,宽8米,长70.6千米,设计加大流量23立方米/秒,到分水岭分为3条干渠,南北纵横,贯穿于林州腹地。红旗渠的成功彻底解决了山区人民用水、吃水的困难。

"自力更生、艰苦创业、团结协作、无私奉献"的红旗渠精神,既是愚公移山精神的延续,又体现了当代中国人的理想信念和不懈追求。勤劳、勇敢、善良的中华儿女,定会将愚公移山精神代代传承。

先秦时期发生在中原地区的六个故事,是中国脍炙人口的历史典故。"周公测影"是周公采用了立表测影的方法寻找大地的中心,"中国"的观念由此奠基、产生。"问鼎中原"楚庄王以问周天子九鼎大小轻重的方式,僭越权力,反映了中原地区自古是兵家必争之地。"孔老问礼"指孔子向老子虚心问礼,体现了儒学和道教思想的交流,树立了后世中华文明的核心和典范。"围魏救赵"是孙膑以围攻魏国的方法解了赵国之围,则反映了战国时期各方势力在中原争相称霸的局面。"杞人忧天"虽是杞人关于天的不切实际的思考,但却体现了人们在早期文明阶段对广袤宇宙的好奇和探索。"愚公移山"的故事流传了千年,更体现出中华儿女坚持不懈的奋斗精神。

feat of water engineering. The Hongqiqu Canal takes the Zhuozhang River as its source of water with the headwork starting from Pingshun County, Shanxi Province. The main canal wall is 4.3 meters high, 8 meters wide and 70.6 kilometers long with a maximum water-channeling capacity of 23 cubic meters per second. The Hongqiqu Canal is divided into three trunk canals in the watershed, running from the south to the north through the hinterland of Linzhou. The successful construction of the Hongqiqu Canal completely solved the problem of water shortage in the mountainous area of Linzhou.

The Hongqiqu Canal spirit of "self-reliance, hard work, solidarity, cooperation and selfless devotion" is not only the continuation of the spirit of "Yugong Removing the Mountains", but also reflects the ideals, beliefs, and unremitting pursuit of contemporary Chinese people. Chinese people who are hardworking, brave and kind-hearted will surely pass on the spirit of "Yugong Removing the Mountains" from generation to generation.

The six stories that took place in the Central Plains during the Pre-Qin period are well-known historical allusions in China. In "Zhou Gong Measuring the Length of the Shadow", Zhou Gong determined the center of the earth by measuring the length of the shadow cast by the sun with a rod erected serving as a measuring stick, from which the concept of "Zhongguo" originated. In "Coveting the Tripods in the Central Plains", King Zhuang of Chu overstepped his power by asking about the size and weight of the nine tripods of the ruler of Zhou, which shows that the Central Plains was a place of strategic importance in ancient China. In "Confucius Asking Laozi About Rites", Confucius visited Laozi and inquired of him about rites with an open mind, reflecting the exchange between Confucianism and Daoism, and establishing the kernel and model of Chinese civilization for later generations. In "Besieging Wei to Rescue Zhao", Sun Bin lifted Zhao out of trouble by besieging Wei, which pictures the vying for hegemony in the Central Plains among various forces during the Warring States Period. Although "The Man of Qi Worrying About the Sky" is about the man's unrealistic thinking about the sky, it reflects people's curiosity about and exploration of the vast universe in the early stage of Chinese civilization. The story of "Yugong Removing the Mountains" has also been passed down for thousands of years, and it is a true reflection of the spirit of unremitting struggle making the Chinese people strong.

第二章

秦汉魏晋南北朝典故

Chapter 2

Allusions in Qin, Han, Wei, Jin, and Southern and Northern Dynasties

秦汉魏晋南北朝时期，包括统一的秦朝和汉朝，以及朝代更迭频繁的三国（魏、蜀、吴）、西晋、东晋和南北朝时期。从公元前221年秦朝建立算起，至公元581年隋朝再次建立起统一王朝，其间一共800多年的历史。秦汉魏晋南北朝时期，河南地区熠熠生辉，有东汉的都城洛阳，有名士辈出的汝南郡（今河南驻马店汝南县），有经济发达的帝乡宛城（今河南南阳宛城区），中原地区是当之无愧的文化、经济、政治的中心。

一、楚河汉界

秦末天下大乱群雄逐鹿，最终以刘邦为首的汉政权和以项羽为首的楚政权脱颖而出。刘项争霸之初，项羽实力雄厚。公元前205年夏，项羽在彭城（今徐州）大败汉军，刘邦退到黄河南岸重镇荥阳，从公元前205年到公元前202年，楚、汉在荥阳展开了长达四年之久的拉锯战。

公元前204年，楚军包围了荥阳，刘邦感到形势危急，向项羽求和。项羽听从谋士范增的计策，拒绝汉军的讲和要求，并决定乘胜追击。刘邦势单兵弱，但非常善用计谋。他接受谋士陈平的建议，对楚军实行反间计，设法离间项羽和范增的关系。项羽虽勇猛却无谋，不知这是刘邦的计策，果然对范增生疑，并把他驱逐出军。范增蒙受不白之冤，含恨离开，途中病死。从此，项羽失去了智多星，贻误战机。

相貌酷似刘邦的大将纪信为解汉王危机，也为了汉军的生存，决定牺牲自己，建议刘邦逃走。刘邦在陈平的劝说下，深被纪信之举所感动，于是让纪信穿上汉王服乘汉王车扮汉王出荥阳东门诈降，自己则趁机从西门出逃至成皋。项羽发现上当后即焚了纪信，攻破成皋。刘邦又迅速从成皋逃出，北渡黄河，军至修武，得到韩信的援助，势力又壮大起来。他接受以往教训，决定采取深沟高垒战术和项羽作持久战，以消耗楚军兵力，同时，又派兵袭楚烧其粮草。

秋天，项羽率兵东进开封、商丘一带作战，留部将曹咎守成皋，并

The period of Qin, Han, Wei, Jin, and Southern and Northern dynasties consists of the unified Qin and Han dynasties, as well as the period of Three Kingdoms (Wei, Shu, Wu), Western Jin, Eastern Jin, and Southern and Northern dynasties during which dynasties changed frequently. From the establishment of the Qin Dynasty in 221 BC to the reestablishment of the unified country by the Sui Dynasty in 581 AD more than 800 years passed. During this period, many places in Henan stood out for different reasons. Luoyang was the capital of the Eastern Han Dynasty. Runan County (now Runan County, Zhumadian, Henan Province) was the birthplace of many famous scholars. Wancheng (now Wancheng District, Nanyang, Henan Province), developed economically and became known as the hometown of an emperor of the Eastern Han Dynasty. During this period, the Central Plains region was indisputably recognized as the cultural, economic and political center of China.

I. The Boundary Between Chu and Han

At the end of the Qin Dynasty, China was in chaos and various great powers vied for hegemony. Two prominent contending powers, Chu led by Xiang Yu, and Han led by Liu Bang, emerged from these principalities and engaged in a struggle for supremacy over China. In the initial stage of the contention between Chu and Han, the Chu army led by Xiang Yu was more powerful. In the summer of 205 BC, the Chu forces were defeated by Xiang Yu in the battle of Pengcheng (now Xuzhou). Liu Bang retreated to Xingyang, an important town on the south bank of the Yellow River. In 205 BC, a four-year seesaw battle started between Chu and Han ending in 202 BC.

In 204 BC, the Chu army besieged Xingyang. Facing a critical and precarious situation, Liu Bang negotiated with Xiang Yu for peace. Xiang Yu, following his adviser Fan Zeng's advice, rejected Liu Bang's proposal and decided to press an attack on Liu Bang's army. Although Liu Bang's army was outnumbered and at a disadvantage, he was very good at using tricks. Taking his adviser Chen Ping's suggestion, Liu Bang took the stratagem of sowing distrust among the Chu army and contrived to drive a wedge between Xiang Yu and Fan Zeng. Being braver than wiser, Xiang Yu didn't realize that this was Liu Bang's trick. As expected, he

楚河汉界

The Boundary Between Chu and Han

再三嘱咐无论如何不要与汉军交锋。汉军得知情报后，多次到城下叫阵，曹咎擅自率部出城，欲渡过汜水与汉军作战，当船至河中时被汉军突袭而败，曹咎后悔不迭，自知无颜见项羽遂自杀身亡。刘邦复取成皋，屯兵广武，取敖仓之粮而用。

项羽闻知成皋失守，急回师广武，刘邦闭城不出。楚军粮食缺乏不利久战，为了迫使刘邦投降，项羽据城东把俘虏来的刘邦的父亲拉至广武山（今霸王城）上，隔涧要挟刘邦说："你若不及早投降，我就把你父亲下锅煮死。"刘邦故作镇静地说："当初咱二人共同反秦，在怀王面前誓盟结为弟兄，我的父亲就是你的父亲。如果你要煮咱们的父亲，

was suspicious of Fan Zeng and expelled him from the army. Wronged by Xiang Yu, Fan Zeng left with resentment and died soon thereafter. As a result, Xiang Yu lost both his wise adviser and combat opportunities.

Ji Xin, a general of Han who resembled Liu Bang, determined to sacrifice his own life for the sake of the survival of the entire Han army and advised Liu Bang to escape. Liu Bang, deeply moved by Ji Xin, and persuaded by Chen Ping, agreed with Ji Xin's suggestion. So Ji Xin pretended to be the king of Han wearing Liu Bang's clothes and rode out of the east gate of Xingyang in Liu Bang's chariot offering surrender to the Chu army. Meanwhile, Liu Bang escaped through the west gate to Chenggao. When Xiang Yu found that he had been fooled, he burned Ji Xin to death and captured Chenggao. Liu Bang was forced to flee from Chenggao and crossed the Yellow River northward to Xiuwu where his power recovered and grew again with the help of Han Xin. Having learned lessons from the past, Liu Bang decided to fight a protracted war with Xiang Yu by digging deep trenches and building high fortresses in order to consume the power of the Chu army. At the same time, he sent troops to attack the Chu army and burn their army provisions.

In the autumn of that year, Xiang Yu led his troops eastward to fight in Kaifeng and Shangqiu, leaving his general Cao Jiu to defend Chenggao. Before leaving, Xiang Yu repeatedly warned Cao jiu not to fight with the Han army. Learning this information, the Han army launched battle outside Chenggao many times. Regardless of Xiang Yu's warning, Cao Jiu was goaded into leading his troops out of the city to cross the Sishui River to fight with the Han army. When their ships reached the middle of the river, they were attacked and defeated by the Han army. Cao Jiu, extremely regretful and too ashamed to see Xiang Yu, committed suicide. After this battle, Liu Bang retook Chenggao, stationed his troops in Guangwu, and used food supplies stored in Aocang.

Learning of the fall of Chenggao, Xiang Yu hurried back to Guangwu only to find Liu Bang closed the city gate, avoiding confrontation with him. The Chu army, short of food supply, was not in a position for a long war. In order to force Liu Bang to surrender, Xiang Yu took Liu Bang's father who was previously captured and held hostage by him to Guangwu mountain (now Bawangcheng) to the east of the city, and threatened Liu Bang across a stream, "If you don't

别忘了给我一碗肉汤。"项羽听后更加恼怒,决定杀掉刘太公。这时,项伯劝项羽道:"杀太公不是时候,也对楚军不利。"项从其言,太公幸存。

项羽虽勇却无谋。此后不久,刘邦兵分两路,一路仍在荥阳同项羽相持,一面派大将韩信抄楚军后路,占领河北、山东一带。从此汉军有了更为巩固的后方,关中的萧何更是源源不断地运来兵员、粮饷。而此时项羽则补给困难,危机四伏,形势发生了逆转,楚军渐弱,汉军日盛。公元前202年秋,楚军粮尽,无奈之下与汉军讲和,双方约定以鸿沟为界"中分天下",以西为汉,以东为楚。这就是历史上著名的"楚汉相争,鸿沟为界"故事的由来。初时刘邦虽然兵力不敌项羽,但在身边谋士的筹谋之下,最终一步步逆天改命,扭转战局,为自己争取最终胜利。项羽虽然勇力过人,但不能知人善任,更是气走唯一谋士范增,可谓是刚愎自用,害人害己。

surrender, I'll boil your father to death." Liu Bang pretended to be calm and said, "During the early days when we two fought together against the Qin Dynasty and swore each other as brothers in the face of King Huai, you said my father was your father. If you want to cook our father today, don't forget to give me a bowl of broth." Hearing this, Xiang Yu became angrier and decided to kill Liu Taigong (Liu Bang's father). At this point, Xiang Bo (Xiang Yu's uncle) advised Xiang Yu, "It's not the right time to kill Taigong, and it is also bad for the Chu army." Xiang Yu took Xiang Bo's advice and Liu Taigong survived.

Brave as Xiang Yu was, he was not wise enough. Not long after, Liu Bang divided his troops into two forces. While one force was still at a stalemate with Xiang Yu's army in Xingyang, the other, under Han Xin's leadership, went to attack the Chu army from the rear and occupied Hebei and Shandong and hence the Han army had a more consolidated home front. In addition, Xiao He in the central Shaanxi plain sent troops and food supplies to them continuously. In contrast, the Chu army was hard-pressed to get supplies and was ridden with crisis. So, the situation was reversed. The Chu army gradually weakened, while the Han army grew increasingly stronger. In the autumn of 202 BC, the Chu army, running out of food, had no choice but to make peace with the Han army. The two sides agreed to "divide the world in the middle" with Honggou as the boundary. The west part of Honggou was assigned as Han territory and the east part as Chu territory. This is the origin of the famous story of "Chu-Han contention ending with Honggou as the boundary" in history. Although Liu Bang was at a disadvantage in the initial stage of the conflict, he managed to turn the tide, reverse the situation with the help of his advisers, and win the final victory. Although Xiang Yu was brave, he couldn't judge and use people well. He even suspected and drove away his only adviser, Fan Zeng. His obstinacy harmed both others and himself.

二、逐鹿中原

在中国文化中，鹿有福禄的寓意，后来逐渐成为政权和帝位的象征。河南省安阳博物馆藏有商王武丁时期"壬申有鹿"（在壬申这一天占卜，问是否能捕获鹿）的卜甲。从殷墟甲骨文和考古发掘来看，商王经常举行以鹿为目标的狩猎活动。作为主要捕猎对象的鹿，逐渐成为王权的象征。"逐鹿中原"的典故便来源于秦末英雄豪杰争夺天下的故事。

逐鹿中原
Chasing the Deer in the Central Plains

II. Chasing the Deer in the Central Plains

In Chinese culture, deer originally were associated with good fortune, and gradually became the symbol of political power and the throne. In the Anyang Museum in Henan Province, there is an oracular shell stating "There are deer on the day of Renshen (the ninth day according to the calendar of Heavenly Stems and Earthly Branches in ancient China)." This shell was used during the period of Wuding (the king of Shang) and it means that the divination practiced on the day of Renshen asked whether one could catch a deer. Judging from the oracle bone inscriptions and archaeological excavations in the Yin Ruins, the king of Shang often held hunting activities with deer as the main object hunted. Therefore, deer gradually became a symbol of supreme royal power. The allusion of "Chasing the Deer in the Central Plains" comes from the story of great forces vying for hegemony at the end of the Qin Dynasty.

In the fourth year of the reign of Emperor Gaozu of Han (203 BC), Han Xin took the kingdom of Qi and was granted the title of king of Qi by Liu Bang, king of the Han Dynasty. Han Xin had made great contributions in the conflict between Chu and Han. Kuai Tong, an advisor to the kingdom of Qi, believed it was Han Xin who would play a pivotal role in the fight for the throne and offered advice to him. In the military commander's tent, Kuai Tong analyzed the situation of the contention between Chu and Han and told Han Xin, "Today, both the fate of the king of Han and that of the king of Chu are in your hands. If you choose to help the king of Han, he will win; if you choose to serve the king of Chu, he will prevail. I'm not sure whether you will take my suggestion, but I'd like to bare my heart to you and offer you sincere advice. It's better to let the king of Chu and the king of Han coexist and you three can form a tripartite balance of forces just like the three legs of a tripod. With the balance of power, no one will dare to take the initiative to launch a war. With your talent and military strength, if you declare yourself independent of Han with Qi as your base and strive for the interest of the people of Qi, all the people will support you. I hope you will seriously consider this issue."

Han Xin replied, "The king of Han treats me so well that my chariots, horses,

汉高祖四年（公元前203年），韩信平定齐国，被汉王刘邦封为齐王。在楚汉之争的过程中，韩信立下了赫赫战功。齐国谋士蒯通认为争夺天下的关键在于韩信，于是为他出谋献计。蒯通在军帐中分析楚汉纷争的局势，对韩信说："当今汉王和项王的命运都掌握在您的手中，您辅佐汉王，则汉王胜利；您为楚王出力，则楚王胜利。我愿意推心置腹，真诚献计，唯恐您不用我的计策。如果能听从我的计策，不如让项王和汉王共同存在下去，与他们三分天下，鼎足而立。这样势力均衡，任何一方都不敢先出兵。凭借您的贤能，以及目前拥有的众多兵力，据守强齐，为民请命，天下必定响应。希望您认真地考虑这件事。"

韩信说："汉王如此厚待于我，我的车马、衣服和食物都是汉王给的。我理应回报汉王的知遇之恩，怎能见利忘义？"蒯通又竭力劝韩信自立为王，指出韩信在汉王手下做事，如若勇略和功绩超过君王，必然会导致杀身之祸。韩信辞谢说："先暂且停止，我将会考虑这件事。"数日后，蒯通再次劝说韩信把握时机以成就功业。韩信犹豫不决，不忍心背叛汉王，又自认为功劳颇大，汉王刘邦不至于夺取他的齐国，于是没有采纳蒯通的建议。

汉高祖五年（公元前202年），刘邦与韩信等约定共击项羽。垓下（今安徽省灵璧县东南）之战，楚军大败，西楚霸王项羽自杀身亡。天下局势逐渐稳定，刘邦看到韩信的势力逐渐扩大，担心韩信将来谋反。韩信知道皇帝畏惧和嫉妒自己的才能，常常称病不朝见，也不随从。

汉高祖十年（公元前197年），陈豨起兵谋反。韩信家臣的弟弟向吕后告发韩信谋反。吕后想要召见韩信，于是和相国萧何共同筹划，假借皇帝的名义召见他，声称陈豨已经死了，让他进宫庆贺。韩信一进宫，吕后就命令武士绑住他，将他斩杀于长乐宫。即将斩

clothes and food are all given by him. I should repay the king of Han for his kindness. How can I disregard moral principles in pursuit of profit?" Kuai Tong still tried to persuade Han Xin to proclaim himself as king independent of Han, pointing out that if Han Xin subordinated himself to the king of Han, once his feats and accomplishments surpassed that of the king of Han, it would inevitably lead to his death. Han Xin expressed his gratitude to Kuai Tong and declined, "Let's drop the topic now and I will consider your advice." A few days later, Kuai Tong once again persuaded Han Xin to seize the opportunity to make some great achievements. But Han Xin hesitated. He was reluctant to betray the king of Han, and believed that in view of the great contributions he had made, Liu Bang, the king of Han, would not seize Qi from him, so he did not adopt Kuai Tong's suggestion.

In the fifth year of the reign of Emperor Gaozu of Han (202 BC), Liu Bang and Han Xin agreed to attack Xiang Yu together. In the battle of Gaixia (now southeast of Lingbi County, Anhui Province), the Chu army was overwhelmingly defeated, and Xiang Yu, the overlord of Western Chu, committed suicide. The situation in China gradually stabilized. Liu Bang, seeing Han Xin's power was expanding, was worried that Han Xin would rebel one day. Han Xin could tell that the emperor was afraid and jealous of his ability, and therefore often avoided meeting the emperor in court or attending to him with the excuse of being ill.

In the 10th year of the reign of Emperor Gaozu of Han (197 BC), Chen Xi launched a rebellion against the Han Dynasty. The younger brother of one of Han Xin's courtiers informed Empress Lv that Han Xin was plotting a rebellion. Empress Lv decided to summon Han Xin. She and the Prime Minister, Xiao He, plotted to lure Han Xin into a trap. They summoned him in the name of the emperor, claiming that Chen Xi had been killed, and Han Xin was invited to Changle Palace for a celebration. The moment Han Xin entered the palace, Empress Lv ordered the guards to bind him and kill him. Just before he was killed, Han Xin said, "How I regret not using Kuai Tong's plan. Now I am deceived by a woman and a villain. Why can't this be the will of Heaven?"

When Liu Bang, Emperor Gaozu of the Han Dynasty, returned to the capital and learned that Han Xin had died, he expressed both glee and regret. He asked, "What did Han Xin say when he died?" Empress Lv answered, "He said he

杀时，韩信说："我后悔不用蒯通的计策，竟然被妇人小子所欺骗，这岂不是天意吗！"

汉高祖刘邦回到京城，见到韩信已经死去，既喜悦又怜惜，问："韩信死时有什么言语？"吕后说："韩信说后悔没有使用蒯通的计谋。"刘邦诏令逮捕蒯通。蒯通到，皇帝说："是你教唆淮阴侯韩信谋反吗？"蒯通回答说："是的，我本来教过他。但是，他没有使用我的计策。如果听从了我的计谋，陛下怎么能杀得了他呢？"皇帝发怒，下令烹杀他。蒯通说："冤枉啊！"皇上说："你教唆韩信谋反，有什么冤枉的？"蒯通回答说："当时秦朝政权崩溃，山东（指函谷关、崤山以东）大乱，异姓诸侯纷纷自立，英雄才俊像乌鸦一样聚集。秦朝丢失了它的鹿，天下人共同追逐它（这里以鹿比喻帝位），才能高且行动敏捷的人先得到。盗贼的狗朝着尧叫，并不是因为尧不仁，而是因为尧不是它的主人。当时我是韩信将军的谋士，只知为韩信筹谋，不知道陛下。况且天下手持精锐兵器想要成为陛下的人众多，只是能力不及您罢了。您又能全部烹杀了他们吗？"刘邦认为蒯通所言有道理，便赦免了他的死罪。

后来，这个故事就凝结为成语"逐鹿中原"，比喻群雄并起，争夺天下。这个成语直观地反映了中原是兵家必争之地，在古代国家政局中占据着不可替代的核心地位。中原是华夏文明的发祥地，自古就有"得中原者得天下"之说。春秋末年便有楚庄王"问鼎中原"的故事。《晋书·石勒载记》记载，石勒说："如果我遇到光武帝，当并驱于中原，不知道鹿会死在谁的手里。"可见，中原长期以来是政治角逐之地。

到魏晋南北朝时期，"中原"一词的地理区域意义最终明晰起来。诸葛亮《出师表》言"北定中原"，将洛阳为中心的地理区域称为中原，当代中原主要是指以河南为主体的地理区域。从夏代到宋代3000多年

regretted not using Kuai Tong's plot." Liu Bang ordered Kuai Tong to be arrested. When Kuai Tong was taken to him, Emperor Gaozu asked, "Did you instigate Han Xin, Lord of Huaiyin, to rebel?" Kuai Tong replied, "Yes, I did give him the suggestion. But he didn't listen to me. If he had followed my plan, how could Your Majesty have killed him?" The emperor was angry and ordered him to be cooked and killed. Kuai Tong said, "I am wronged!" The emperor said, "How dare you claim you are wronged since you abetted Han Xin to rebel?" Kuai Tong replied, "When the Qin Dynasty collapsed, Shandong (referring to the region to the east of Hangu Pass and Xiaoshan Mountain) was in chaos. Various principalities declared themselves as independent, and heroes gathered like crows. The ruler of the Qin Dynasty lost his deer, and people all over the country chased it. (Here, deer stands for the throne) But only those with great abilities and quick action can get it before others. The thief's dog barked at Yao, not because Yao was unkind, but because Yao was not its owner. At that time, since I was an advisor serving General Han Xin, it was my duty to make plans for him, but not for you Your Majesty. Moreover, there are so many people with elite weapons who want to take Your Majesty's position. They failed just because they are not so capable as you are. Can you cook and kill all of them?" Seeing some point in Kuai Tong's words, Liu Bang spared his life.

Later, this story was condensed into the idiom "Chasing the Deer in the Central Plains", which means that all heroes rise to vie for the throne. This idiom directly shows that the Central Plains is a place of strategic importance and has an irreplaceable core position in the political landscape of ancient China. The Central Plains is the birthplace of Chinese civilization. Since ancient times, there has been the saying that those who get the Central Plains can rule China. There was also the story of King Zhuang of Chu "Coveting the Tripods in the Central Plains" at the end of the Spring and Autumn Period. In the "Records of Shi Le" in the *Book of Jin*, Shi Le said, "If I lived in the same period as Emperor Guangwu, I would fight with him in the Central Plains. It's hard to say who would kill the deer (who would be the winner and get the throne)." All this shows that the Central Plains has long been a place of political competition in Chinese history.

By the period of Wei, Jin, and Southern and Northern dynasties, the geographical significance of the Central Plains was finally clarified. Zhuge Liang

间,河南一直是中国的政治、经济和文化中心,并创造了灿烂的中原文化。"逐鹿中原"的典故,显示了中原在古代中国的重要地位,证明了中原文明在中华文明中的核心地位。

quoted it, saying "to conquer the northern heartland in the Central Plains" in *Chu Shi Biao* (*Marching Remarks*) where he designated the geographical area with Luoyang at the center as the Central Plains. The Central Plains today is mainly a geographical area with Henan as the main body. For more than 3000 years from the Xia Dynasty to the Song Dynasty, Henan was China's political, economic and cultural center, where a splendid Central Plains culture was created. The allusion of "Chasing the Deer in the Central Plains" shows the important position of the Central Plains in ancient China and testifies to the core status of the Central Plains to Chinese civilization.

三、白马驮经

佛教于东汉初传入中国。河南地处中原，是中华文明的主要发源地之一，也是佛教在我国内地传播最早的地方之一，河南佛教在中国佛教历史上占有极其重要的地位。永平十一年（公元 68 年），汉明帝在洛阳修建了中国最早的佛教寺院——白马寺。

白马寺位于洛阳市洛龙区洛白路，为中国第一古刹、世界著名伽蓝，是佛教传入我国后官办的第一座寺院，被中外佛教界誉为"释源"（释教之发源）、"祖庭"（祖师之庭院）、"中国第一古刹"。直到今天，白马寺保存下来的古代碑刻和供器上，都还留有"祖庭"和"释源"字样。这就使洛阳白马寺和其他任何一座佛寺都有所区别，从而在中国佛教史上占有独特的地位。佛教虽起源于印度，但发展却在中国。汉魏之后，中国佛法日隆。由河洛至江汉，由繁华京师至穷乡僻壤，九州起庙，五岳树塔，"金刹与灵台比高，广殿共阿房等壮"，此皆始于汉明帝创建之白马寺。

东汉永平七年（公元 64 年），正月十五元宵佳节（或云四月八日）。汉明帝刘庄（刘秀之子）夜寐南宫，梦见一个高大的金人，身长丈六，自西方而来，在殿庭上飞绕。第二天早晨，汉明帝召集大臣，告其所梦。傅毅启奏道："臣闻西方有神，名曰佛，形如陛下所梦者。"汉明帝听了之后信以为真，便派大臣蔡愔、秦景等十余人，出使西域，拜求佛经、佛法。

永平八年（公元 65 年），蔡、秦等东汉使者告别帝都，踏上了"西天取经"的万里征途，越过旷无人烟、寸草不生的八百里流沙，攀上寒风驱雁、飞雪千里的茫茫葱岭，来到大月氏国（今阿富汗境至中亚一带），刚好遇到正在当地游化宣教的印度高僧、佛学大师摄摩腾、竺法兰，得见佛经和释迦牟尼佛像，恳请腾、兰二高僧东赴中国弘法宣教。

III. The White Horse Carrying Buddhist Sutras

Buddhism was introduced into China in the early Eastern Han Dynasty. Henan, located in the Central Plains, is one of the birthplaces of Chinese civilization and also one of the places in the mainland of China where Buddhism was first disseminated. Henan Buddhism takes an important position in the history of Chinese Buddhism. In the 11th year of the Yongping reign (68 AD), Emperor Ming of the Han Dynasty ordered the building of the earliest Buddhist temple in China—the Baima Temple in Luoyang.

Located in Luobai Road, Luolong District, Luoyang City, Baima Temple is the first Buddhist temple in China and a world-famous Sangharama (monastic grounds). It is the first official temple after Buddhism was introduced into China. It is also known as "Shiyuan (Cradle of Buddhism)", "Zuting (Founder's Home)" and "the first ancient temple in China" in domestic and international Buddhist circles. Down to the present, such characters as " 祖庭 " and " 释源 " can still be found on the ancient inscriptions and sacrificial vessels preserved in Baima Temple. This sets Baima Temple of Luoyang apart from any other Buddhist temples, putting it in a unique position in the history of Chinese Buddhism. Although Buddhism originated in India, it developed in China. After the Han and Wei dynasties, Chinese Buddhism began to flourish. From Heluo to Jianghan, from the prosperous capital to remote and poor areas, temples and towers were built in every corner of China. "The golden temples are as high as the Astronomical Observation Tower (built in the Zhou Dynasty), and the spacious halls are as magnificent as Epang Palace (built in the Qin Dynasty)". Such a situation started with Baima Temple founded by Emperor Ming of the Han Dynasty.

In the seventh year of Yongping reign of the Eastern Han Dynasty (64 AD), on the day of the Lantern Festival (or the 8th of April according to another version of the story), Emperor Ming of the Han Dynasty, Liu Zhuang (son of Liu Xiu), slept in the south palace at night and dreamed of a gold man, six *zhangs* (20 meters) tall, coming from the west and flying around the court. The next morning, Emperor Ming summoned his courtiers and told them about his dream. Fu Yi said, "I've been told that there is a God in the west named Buddha, who looks just

第二章　秦汉魏晋南北朝典故

永平十年（公元 67 年），二位印度高僧应邀和东汉使者一道，用白马驮载佛经、佛像同返国都洛阳。汉明帝见到佛经、佛像，十分高兴，对二位高僧极为礼重，亲自予以接待，并安排他们在当时负责外交事务的官署"鸿胪寺"暂住。

翌年，汉明帝敕令于洛阳城西雍门外三里御道北兴修僧院。"于其壁，画千乘万骑，绕塔三匝，又于南宫清凉台及开阳门上作佛像"，为纪念白马驮经，取名"白马寺"。这就在东土大地，周、孔、老、庄之

白马驮经
The White Horse Carrying Buddhist Sutras

like the one Your Majesty have dreamed of." Emperor Ming believed what Fu Yi said and sent more than ten of his subjects including Cai Yin and Qin Jing to the Western Regions to pray for the Buddhist scriptures and Dharma.

In the eighth year of Yongping reign (65 AD), Cai Yin, Qin Jing and other envoys of the Eastern Han Dynasty left the imperial capital and embarked on the long journey of "getting the scriptures from the west". Crossing the vast quicksand area which was barren and desolate, climbing the formidable Congling (the Pamirs) covered with white snow where the wild geese flew away for fear of the cold wind, they finally arrived in the great Yuezhi country (now the region from the border of Afghanistan to Central Asia), just in time to meet She Moteng (Kasyapa Matanga) and Zhu Falan (Dharmaranya), the eminent Indian monks and Buddhist masters who were traveling around and preaching in the local area. After seeing the Buddhist scriptures and the statue of Sakyamuni Buddha, they implored the two eminent monks to travel east to China to preach and promote the Dharma.

In the 10th year of Yongping reign (67 AD), the two eminent Indian monks, accepting the invitation, returned to Luoyang with envoys of the Eastern Han Dynasty. They brought with them a white horse loaded with Buddhist sutras and statues. Emperor Ming of the Han Dynasty was very happy to see the Buddhist scriptures and statues. He showed great reverence to the two eminent monks, received them personally, and arranged for them to stay in Honglu Temple, the official office in charge of foreign affairs at that time.

In the following year, Emperor Ming of the Han Dynasty ordered the building of a monastery in the north of Sanliyudao (the imperial avenue) outside Xiyong Gate of Luoyang City. "Thousands of horses and chariots that are going around the tower three times are drawn on its wall, and statues of Buddha are made on the Kaiyang Gate and Qingliang Tai (the cool and clear terrace) of the south palace". It was given the name Baima Temple (White Horse Temple) in commemoration of the horse's arduous task of carrying the Buddhist sutras. Hence, the earliest Buddhist temple in China was erected in the vast territory right by the side of Luohe River in the capital city of the Han Dynasty which is also the hometown of such great figures as Zhou Gong (the Duke of Zhou), Confucius, Laozi and Zhuangzi. Shortly thereafter, Emperor Ming of the Han Dynasty ordered the construction of the Qiyun Pagoda.

邦，洛河之滨，天子脚下，诞生了中国最早的一座佛寺——洛阳白马寺。此后不久，汉明帝又敕令兴建齐云塔。

摄摩腾和竺法兰在此译出《四十二章经》，此为现存中国第一部汉译佛典。在摄摩腾和竺法兰之后，又有多位西方高僧来到白马寺译经。在公元68年以后的一百五十多年里，有一百九十二部，合计三百九十五卷佛经在这里译出，白马寺成为当之无愧的中国第一译经道场。

曹魏嘉平二年（公元250年），印度高僧昙柯迦罗来到白马寺。此时佛教也从深宫走进了市井民间。随后，昙柯迦罗在白马寺译出了第一部汉文佛教戒律《僧祇戒心》。同一时期，安息国僧人昙谛，也在白马寺译出了规范僧团组织生活的《昙无德羯磨》。至此，戒律和僧团组织章程都已齐备，一条中土有缘人出家持戒修行的道路铺就，为中土戒律之始。

曹魏甘露五年（公元260年），一场受戒仪式在白马寺举行，这是一个注定要深深印刻在中国佛教史上的事件。这一天，朱士行依《羯磨法》登上戒坛，跪于佛祖面前，成了中国汉地第一位正式受过比丘戒的出家人。自此，儒家"身体发肤，受之父母，不敢毁伤"的古老传统被打破了。

佛教在中国扎根、传播最初的二百年，整个过程都与白马寺息息相关。这里是中国第一次西天求法的产物，是最早来中国传教弘法的僧人的居所；这里诞生了第一部中文佛经和中文戒律，出现了第一个中国汉地僧人……总之，白马寺是与中国佛教的许多个"第一"紧紧联系在一起的，这让它成为名副其实的中国佛教的祖庭和释源。

In Baima Temple, She Moteng and Zhu Falan translated the first Buddhist scripture into Chinese from Sanskrit: *The Sutra in Forty-two Sections Spoken by the Buddha*. Afterwards, many eminent monks from the west came to Baima Temple to translate scriptures. During the 150-plus years after 68 AD, altogether 192 Buddhist scriptures, totaling 395 volumes, were translated in Baima Temple and it earned the well-deserved status of the first Sutra translation center in China.

In the second year of the reign of the Caowei Emperor Jiaping (250 AD), an Indian monk, Tan Kejialuo, came to Baima Temple. By then, Buddhism had been popularized and well-accepted among ordinary Chinese people. In Baima Temple, Tan Kejialuo translated the first commandment into Chinese entitled *Buddhist Disciplines for Monks*. In the same period, Tan Di, a monk from the Empire of Anxi (Parthian Empire), also in Baima Temple, finished the translation of *Tanwude Karma*, which regulates the life of Buddhist groups. The commandments and rules of Chinese Buddhist groups were established, paving the way for the Chinese people to convert to Buddhism and practice the commandments. This is the beginning of the Buddhist commandments in China.

In the fifth year of the reign of the Caowei Emperor Ganlu (260 AD), a Buddhist initiation ritual was held in Baima Temple, which was later to be engraved in the history of Chinese Buddhism. On this day, Zhu Shixing ascended the ordination platform in accordance with the *Law of Karma*, knelt down before the Sakyamuni Buddha, and became the first Chinese converting to Buddhism in the Han Dynasty to officially receive full ordination. With his ordination, the ancient Confucian tradition of "my body, hair and skin are given by my parents and cannot be damaged" was broken.

In the first 200 years after Buddhism was introduced into China, it was all via Baima Temple that Buddhism took root and then it started to spread in China. This temple is the product of the first journey of Chinese to the west to pray for Buddhism, and the residence of the first community of monks who came to China to preach and promote the Dharma. It was here that the first Chinese Buddhist scriptures and commandments were created and the first Chinese Buddhist monk appeared. In short, Baima Temple is closely linked with many "firsts" in the development of Chinese Buddhism, which makes it the "Founder's Home" and the "Cradle of Buddhism" in China in the real sense.

四、三顾茅庐

世人只知滴水可穿石而感叹这点点滴滴的水珠的奥妙，殊不知穿透石头的不是那最后一滴，而是它们中的每一滴。没有经年累月连续不断的滴落，又哪有如今的水滴石穿。在这小小的水滴背后，蕴含着一种坚持不懈的精神，可谓是锲而不舍，金石可镂。同样坚持不懈也是中华民族的传统美德。在中国历史的长河中，这种通过自己的坚持最终达到目的的故事屡见不鲜，三顾茅庐就是其中一个。故事中的主人公就如同司汤达说的那样，"一个人只要强烈地坚持不懈地追求，他就能达到目的"。

三顾茅庐

Three Visits to Zhuge Liang's Thatched Cottage

IV. Three Visits to Zhuge Liang's Thatched Cottage

The world only knows that drops of water can penetrate stones and exclaims at the mystery of these little drops of water. In fact, it is not the last drop that penetrates the stone, but each of them does so. Without years of dripping, how can the stone be worn away? Behind these small droplets of water is the spirit of perseverance which can engrave gold and diamond. Perseverance is also a traditional virtue of the Chinese people. In the long run of Chinese history, it is not uncommon to hear stories of people reaching their goals through perseverance, and the story of "Three Visits to Zhuge Liang's Thatched Cottage" is one of them. As Stendhal said, "A man can achieve his goal as long as he pursues it with intense perseverance." This story, which is set in Nanyang City, Henan Province, displays the protagonist living up to this virtue.

At the end of the Eastern Han Dynasty, eunuchs had absolute power. The world was in chaos and the political situation was in such turbulence that heroes from all walks of life rose up one after another. Liu Bei was from the imperial clan of the Han Dynasty and in the years of warfare, many wise and able men came to join him. He himself loved the wise and he went around to seek the talents. At that time, Cao Cao set up a separatist regime in the north. Though much more powerful than Liu Bei, Cao Cao still regarded him as a threat and schemed to win to his side Liu Bei's henchmen and counselors. Among Liu Bei's counselors was a man named Xu Shu. Cao Cao captured his mother and forced him to abandon Liu Bei. Before leaving for Cao Cao's camp, Xu Shu recommended Zhuge Liang to Liu Bei and said that whoever won the help of Zhuge Liang would win the world. Then what on earth was Zhuge Liang like?

Zhuge Liang (181 AD-234 AD), also known as Kongming, lost his father at an early age and after that he went to Jingzhou with his uncle. After his uncle's death, he retired to Wolong in Longzhong (now Dengzhou, Nanyang, Henan Province). Zhuge Liang was about eight feet tall, very handsome and had displayed unusual talents since he was a child. He was well-informed, erudite, and knew well the world's great events. He compared himself to Guan Zhong, the governor of the State of Qi of the Spring and Autumn Period, and Yue

这个故事就发生在河南省南阳市。

东汉末年，宦官专权，天下大乱，政治局势浩荡，全国各路英雄纷纷起兵。刘备是汉朝的宗室，起兵多年，很多能人志士都来投靠他。他本人也礼贤下士，四处求访人才。当时，曹操割据北方，认为刘备势力虽小，但仍能威胁到自己，便想方设法地将他身边的亲信和谋士夺取过来。在刘备的众多谋士中有个叫作徐庶的谋士，曹操抓获了徐庶的母亲，使他不得不离开刘备。但徐庶临走前向刘备举荐诸葛亮，说诸葛亮是天下难得的奇才，谁得到他的相助，这天下就是谁的。那诸葛亮到底是何许人也？

诸葛亮（公元181年—公元234年），字孔明，早年丧父，后随叔父到荆州，叔父去世后，他便在隆中（今河南南阳邓州）卧龙岗结庐隐居下来。诸葛亮身高八尺，容貌非常英俊，从小就表现出异于常人的才华。他饱览群书，学问渊博，并且对天下大事了然于心。他常常将自己比作春秋战国时期的管仲（春秋时齐国名相）和乐毅（战国时燕国名将），但当时的人都不承认，只有与诸葛亮关系较好的人认为他很了不起。

当时刘备在新野（今河南南阳新野县）听了徐庶的介绍后，便说让徐庶带上诸葛亮来见他。徐庶说道："若想要此人相助，只能将军你屈尊亲自去拜访，切不可委屈了他。"刘备也很虚心受教，决定亲自去拜会诸葛亮。

第二天刘备便同关羽和张飞带着礼物，连夜赶往隆中，拜访诸葛亮。看门的小童听说他们来找自己的主人，便告知他们先生不在家，早上便出门了，不知道先生什么时候才会回来。刘备只好失望地离开隆中。虽然这次没有见到诸葛亮，但刘备并未就此放弃。

过了几天，刘备打听到诸葛亮已经回到家中，便又同关羽和张飞前去拜访。三人顶着漫天飞雪赶到隆中，却被告知诸葛亮在前一天就和朋友一同出去云游了。尽管连着两次都没有见到诸葛亮，刘备仍未生气，依然坚持。

又过了些时间，刘备准备第三次去拜访诸葛亮。此时关羽和张飞都

Yi, a famous general of the Warring States Period, but few people of his time acknowledged his great talent except several of his close friends.

At that time Liu Bei was in Xinye (Xinye County, Nanyang, Henan). Having heard Xu Shu's introduction to Zhuge Liang, he asked Xu Shu to bring Zhuge Liang to him. "If you ask for this man's help," Xu Shu said, "you must pay him a personal visit." Liu Bei was very humble and he decided to visit Zhuge Liang in person.

The next day, Liu Bei, together with Guan Yu and Zhang Fei, took gifts and rushed to Longzhong overnight to visit Zhuge Liang. They were greeted by a little doorman who told them that his master had gone out that morning, and that he did not know when his master would return. Although he was unable to see Zhuge Liang this time, Liu Bei was not discouraged.

A few days later when Liu Bei was informed that Zhuge Liang had returned, he went to Longzhong again with Guan and Zhang. They arrived in Longzhong under a heavy snowfall, only to be told that Zhuge Liang had gone out with a friend to travel around the day before. Although he failed to see Zhuge Liang a second time, he did not get angry and decided not to give up.

Some time passed and Liu Bei prepared to pay a third visit to Zhuge. Guan and Zhang harbored anger already about meeting Zhuge, but Liu Bei did not lose heart. When they all returned to Wolong, a boy told them that his master was sleeping. Liu Bei stood respectfully at the bottom of the steps outside the thatched cottage and waited. After Zhuge Liang awoke, he immediately asked Liu Bei to come in.

Once they had introduced themselves to each other, Liu Bei asked Zhuge Liang what he could do to bring peace to the world, and expressed his own determination and willingness to give his people a good life. Impressed by Liu Bei's modesty and sincerity, Zhuge Liang analysed the world's situation for Liu Bei and recommended a strategy of allying with Sun Quan in the east, resisting Cao Cao in the north, and occupying Sichuan so that the world could be united step by step. Liu Bei was enlightened by Zhuge Liang's vision for his future, and from that time forward, his relationship with Zhuge Liang became increasingly close, to the dismay of both Guan Yu and Zhang Fei. Liu Bei persuaded them, saying, "With the help of Zhuge Liang, I feel like a fish in the water. I hope

已有怒气，但刘备并不灰心。三人再次来到卧龙岗，听小童说先生正在睡觉，刘备便毕恭毕敬地站在草堂外的台阶下静静等候。诸葛亮醒后立即将刘备请进屋中。

进屋后，二人互相介绍完自己的身份，刘备便向诸葛亮询问关于平定天下事的对策，并且表明想让百姓过上好日子的决心和意愿。诸葛亮见刘备谦虚诚恳，便向他分析天下形势并制订了东联孙吴、北拒曹操、袭据四川、徐图统一的战略计划。刘备听完诸葛亮为他描绘的宏图大业后，茅塞顿开，自此和诸葛亮的关系日益密切，使得关羽和张飞等人心生不满。刘备劝解他们说："我有了诸葛亮相助，如鱼得水，希望你们勿要再对他心生芥蒂。"后来刘备与诸葛亮谈论天下事的这段佳话也被称为"隆中对"。

刘备被诸葛亮的聪明才智折服，随即便提出想请他相助的意愿。诸葛亮也不推辞，当即便随刘备回新野，此后更是用尽自己毕生的智慧帮其打天下：先是帮助刘备发展壮大军队，为后来的争霸天下积蓄力量；后又主动出使东吴，说服孙权联合刘备抵抗曹操，取得了赤壁大战的胜利；接着，又协助刘备占领了荆州的大部分地区，夺取了益州，形成了三分天下的战略格局，进入三国鼎立时期，一步步践行当日"隆中对策"的计划。魏黄初二年（公元221年），刘备称帝，国号为汉，诸葛亮为丞相。刘备临终前将国家大事托付给他，希望他能辅佐幼帝来继承尚未完成的大业。诸葛亮也没有辜负刘备对他的期望，为了实现光复汉室的宏图大业，鞠躬尽瘁，死而后已。

坚持不懈自古以来就是中华民族自强不息、顽强拼搏的优良传统美德。也正是刘备的坚持，才让他等到诸葛亮这个贤才，使他在三国争霸中有一席之地。三顾茅庐这个故事让我们看到了坚持的精神，刘备礼贤下士和招贤纳才的行为也让我们看到了中国古代惜才的人才观。同样对诸葛亮来说，刘备对他有知遇之恩，在他的身上我们也能看出中国古代文人志士"士为知己者死"的高尚情操。

you bear him no grudge." This much-told story was later known as "Meeting at Longzhong".

Impressed by Zhuge Liang's ingenuity, Liu Bei immediately invited him for help, and without declining Liu Bei's invitation, Zhuge followed Liu Bei back to Xinye right away. Ever since then, Zhuge had committed his life to helping Liu Bei to conquer the world. First, he helped Liu Bei develop and expand his army and build up strength for the struggle for supremacy. Then, he sent an envoy to Eastern Wu to make an alliance against Cao Cao resulting in a victory in the battle at Chibi. He also helped Liu Bei occupy most of Jingzhou and seize Yizhou, forming a strategic pattern of a tripartite world and moving China into the period of the Three Kingdoms. Step by step, they implemented the plan they made at Longzhong. In 221 AD, the second year of Huangchu of Wei, Liu Bei proclaimed himself Emperor with the title of Han and appointed Zhuge Liang as Prime Minister. Before his death, Liu Bei entrusted Zhuge Liang with the state affairs, hoping that he could assist the new young emperor to continue the unfinished causes of Liu Bei. Without letting his master down, Zhuge Liang devoted his life to recovering the reign of Han until he died.

Perseverance has been a traditional virtue of Chinese people. Owing to Liu Bei's persistence, he won the support of Zhuge Liang with whose help he established his political power in the Three Kingdoms Period. The story of Liu Bei's three visits to Zhuge Liang helps us see how Liu Bei valued the talented and persisted in seeking the wise. As for Zhuge Liang, he embodies the high-mindedness of the ancient Chinese literati and heroes who die for those who know themselves.

五、老骥伏枥

中国拥有悠久的历史文化,而梦想是悠久历史文化的重要组成部分。《大学》用"三纲领"和"八条目"描述儒生的梦想,"明德""亲民""止于至善"三者被称为《大学》的"三纲领","格物""致知""诚意""正心""修身""齐家""治国""平天下"八者被称为《大学》的"八条目"。无论古今,人们对梦想总是怀着无限的憧憬和坚定的信念,在古人对梦想的表述中,老骥伏枥是其中非常有代表性的故事,而现今中国梦思想的提出也是希望人们要为梦想奋斗终生。

老骥伏枥

The Old Steed over the Manger

光武帝刘秀建立东汉初期,经过多年的统一战争,结束了王莽新朝末年的军阀混战与割据局面。国泰民安,人民幸福,刘秀在位期间,大兴儒学、推崇气节、柔道治国、大兴水利,号称"建武盛世"。然而到了汉灵帝时,东汉已逐渐呈现衰败崩溃之势,政治动荡,诸侯四起,天下大乱,其中以曹操

V. The Old Steed over the Manger

China is a country with a long history and rich culture, and dreams are an integral part of its story. The classic *Great Learning* describes the Confucian dreams by offering three creeds—"virtue", "affinity", and "supreme good", and eight goals—"studying things", "seeking knowledge", "sincerity", "integrity", "self-cultivation", "raising family", "governing the country", and "pacifying the world". Whether they are ancient or modern, Chinese people always have an unlimited vision and firm belief in dreams. Of the ancient stories about dreams, "An Old Steed over the Manger" is a representative. Likewise, the current concept of the Chinese Dream has been put forward with a wish that all Chinese people shall struggle to achieve their dreams all their lives.

In the early Eastern Han Dynasty established by Liu Xiu, Emperor Guangwu, the situation of warlords vying for power ended after many years of war in the last years of Wang Mang's Dynasty. The rule of Liu Xiu, called the flourishing age, witnessed peace and prosperity. Confucianism was blooming, moral integrity was championed, the country was governed with mercy, and water conservancy was built. When it came to Emperor Ling of Han, the rule of the Eastern Han Dynasty began to decline with feudal vassals rising up from all directions among whom Cao Cao was the most far-sighted. Cao Cao (155 AD-220 AD), literary name Mengde, born in Qiao County of the Pei State, today's Bo County of Anhui Province, was once elected as Xiaolian. He joined military actions against Dong Zhuo, defeated and incorporated the Yellow Turban Army and established a Qingzhou army. He dreamed of unifying the country and re-establishing a stable society.

In 196 AD, the first year of Jian'an, Emperor Xian of Han, Cao Cao moved the headquarter of the Han Dynasty to Xu (present-day east of Xuchang, Henan Province), where he launched the garrison reclamation system. Under this system, the soldiers or people were organized to grow crops to ensure army provisions. During the period of war, food was in short supply and robbers rose in rebellion. To keep the society stable, Cao Cao ordered soldiers to do the farming and extended this system to every county so that the situation of food shortage was lessened.

最有远见。曹操（公元155年—公元220年），字孟德，沛国谯县（今安徽亳州市）人，初举孝廉为郎，参与了讨伐董卓之役，并击败、收编青州黄巾军，建立青州兵。他希望统一天下，重新建立安定的社会。

汉献帝建安元年（公元196年），曹操迁汉献帝于许（今河南许昌东），开始在许下屯田。屯田是利用士兵或招募百姓耕种荒地以保证军粮供应的一种措施，当时各地遭受战乱，到处都缺乏粮食，各地豪强同时起兵。为了稳定秩序，曹操下令屯田，并且逐步把屯田制度推广到各州郡，缓解了当时谷物匮乏的局势。

许昌屯田以后，曹操先后消灭了董卓、黄巾军、袁绍等地方势力，基本上统一了北方。汉献帝建安五年（公元200年），曹操在官渡（今河南省中牟县）之战中，以少胜多，大败袁绍。从此，军威大振，曹操更加雄心勃勃。但是，袁绍的两个儿子投奔了乌桓，企图借助乌桓的力量重建自己的势力。乌桓的经济、文化较落后，由于中原地区经常混战，所以它多次侵袭汉朝的领土，北方人民的生命财产没有保障。对此，曹操决心征讨乌桓。汉献帝建安十二年（公元207年），曹操亲自统帅大军北上远征乌桓。当时曹操已年过半百，古人认为，人到50岁，基本就进入衰老阶段，这点曹操心里也十分清楚，但曹操仍然胸怀壮志，人老心不老。他驰骋疆场，力图彻底消灭袁氏残余势力，真正统一北方。经过长达几个月的艰苦行军作战，曹操在白狼山（今辽宁省朝阳市大阳山）一带与乌桓进行了激烈的争战，彻底击败了乌桓，杀死了他们的头领，使乌桓十几万人被迫投降。

曹操率领大军凯旋，在返回的路上，曹操带着胜利的喜悦，想着自己虽然年过半百，但身负历史重任，因为统一中原的大业尚未完成，自己的雄心壮志还没有实现。于是他激情澎湃，赋诗一首，名为《步出夏门行·龟虽寿》。诗云："神龟虽寿，犹有竟时。腾蛇乘雾，终为土灰。老骥伏枥，志在千里；烈士暮年，壮心不已。"典故老骥伏枥就出自此诗，老骥伏枥的意思是说，年老力衰的千里马虽卧躺在马槽边，却仍然

This system strengthened the power of Emperor Xian and enabled Cao Cao to subdue the local powers of Dong Zhuo, Yuan Shao and the Yellow Turban Army, almost unifying the north into one state. In 200 AD, the fifth year of Jian'an, although outnumbered, Cao Cao nevertheless defeated Yuan Shao at Guandu (now Zhongmu in Henan). With his military power hence greatly enhanced, Cao Cao became more ambitious. However, Yuan Shao's two sons fled to Wuhuan for shelter, thinking of rebuilding their power with the help of the Wuhuan ethnic group (in today's Inner Mongolia). Wuhuan was economically and culturally backward, and because the Central Plains was often in turbulence, Wuhuan repeatedly invaded the territory of Han, and the lives and property of the people in the north were not safe. In response, Cao Cao was determined to conquer Wuhuan. In 207 AD, the 12th year of Emperor Xian, Cao Cao led an army and marched North for Wuhuan. At that time, Cao Cao was already in his fifties, and it was believed that when people reached the age of 50, they basically entered the stage of aging. Cao Cao was very clear about it in his heart, but he still had ambitions and was not discouraged by the old age. He galloped across the battlefield, trying to wipe out the remnants of the Yuan forces and realize a true reunification of the north. After several months of arduous marching, Cao Cao got engaged in a fierce battle with the Wuhuan people around White Wolf Mountain (in present-day Dayang Mountain, Chaoyang, Liaoning Province). He completely defeated Wuhuan, killed their leaders, and forced more than 100,000 Wuhuan people to surrender.

Leading his army back from his triumph, Cao Cao was filled with the joy of victory, thinking that although he was over 50 years old, he still bore an important historical responsibility. The great cause of unifying the Central Plains had not been completed, and his own dreams had not yet come true. Inspired by his passion, he wrote a poem named *"Stepping out of the Summer Gate · Long-lived as Turtles"*. The poem says, "Long-lived are turtles, yet they are mortal; snakes ride the clouds, all ending in dust; the old steed chews over the manger, aiming at running another thousand miles; though warriors are old, they cease not to fight." The allusion of "The Old Steed over the Manger" is included in this poem, meaning that although the steed is old and weak, it still dreams of galloping another journey to the battle. Comparing himself to the old horse, Cao Cao meant to express his will of moving on to fulfill his dreams of changing the world and unifying the Central Plains in spite of his old age. This allusion is now frequently used to refer to persons with

拥有着驰骋千里的雄心壮志，曹操想用老骥伏枥来抒发自己的雄心壮志。老骥伏枥表现了曹操老当益壮、志在千里的积极进取精神，抒发了他变革现实、统一中原的豪情壮志。后人常以老骥伏枥来比喻有志之士，年纪虽老而仍有雄心壮志，为梦想奋斗终生。

在历史的长河中，古人为梦想奋斗终生的例子还有许多。例如，张骞不畏艰险多次出使西域。张骞是中国汉代杰出的外交家、丝绸之路的开拓者，为了联合西域各国共同抗击匈奴，张骞多次出使西域。这体现了他为实现梦想而奋斗终生的追求。又如唐朝文学家王勃在《滕王阁序》中写道："老当益壮，宁移白首之心？穷且益坚，不坠青云之志。"人虽然年老，但志气应当更加旺盛，不能在年老时改变心境，境遇虽然困苦，但节操应当更加坚定，绝不能抛弃自己的凌云壮志。后人列举这些事迹的意义是希望人们拥有积极向上的人生精神，就像典故老骥伏枥展示的那样，虽然有时候一些因素是不能控制的，人们还是要为梦想奋斗终生。

老骥伏枥这个典故的中心意思是为梦想奋斗终生，同时反映了中国古人对梦想的追求。梦想是人生的导航，是奋斗让梦想成为现实。人们在为梦想奋斗的过程中会发现人生的意义，无论古今人们都在为实现这个目标而奋斗。

秦汉魏晋南北朝的历史典故以争夺天下为背景，反映了中原作为国家政治、经济、文化中心的历史地位。"楚河汉界"中刘邦率领的汉军和项羽统帅的楚军，以鸿沟为界争夺天下，最后以刘邦的胜利而告终。"逐鹿中原"则以刘邦杀韩信为线索，展现了当时群雄并起、争夺天下的态势。"白马驮经"是指汉明帝派使者去往印度取经，体现了中原文化兼容并包、海纳百川的鲜明特点。"三顾茅庐"和"老骥伏枥"两个典故发生在魏晋南北朝时期大分裂的历史背景下，刘备、曹操都有一统天下的抱负，典故中所体现的礼贤下士、老当益壮的精神，至今仍为人们所津津乐道。

lofty minds of working for their purposes all their lives.

In the long run of history, there are many examples of this kind. Take Zhang Qian for another example. Zhang Qian was an outstanding diplomat of the Han Dynasty and a pioneer of the Silk Road. In order to unite the countries of the Western Regions to jointly fight against Xiongnu, Zhang Qian was sent on many missions to the Western Regions. Subduing the Western Regions was his lifelong dream. Again, think of Wang Bo, a poet of the Tang Dynasty, and his poem, *Preface to Tengwang Pavilion* in which he writes, "Shall white hair impale your heart? How could adversity undermine your aspiration?" Let your ambition not die away but be strengthened with old age; hard times shall not eat away your high spirit but highlight it. Allusions like "The Old Steed over the Manger" convey to us the message that we shall embrace an optimistic view toward life despite the uncontrolled environment.

The allusion of "The Old Steed over the Manger" chiefly means the never-ceasing struggle to pursue one's dreams, embodying ancient Chinese people's aspiration to achieve their life goals. Goals and dreams are the guidance of life. If there is no struggle, no dreams will come true. People will find the meaning of life in the process of striving for their dreams, and this effort has never ceased in the long run of history.

The historical allusions of the Qin, Han, Wei, Jin, and Southern and Northern dynasties, set in the context of the struggle for the control of the world, reflect the Central Plains' historical status as the country's political, economic and cultural center. "The Boundary Between Chu and Han" bears witness to the war between Liu Bang from Han and Xiang Yu from Chu along Honggou, the border which ended with Liu Bang's victory. "Chasing the Deer in the Central Plains" comes from the story of Liu Bang killing Han Xin, and it aims to reveal the situation of heroes rising up for control of the world. "The White Horse Carrying Buddhist Sutras" refers to the story of Emperor Ming of Han sending envoys to India to fetch Buddhist scriptures, reflecting the inclusiveness of the culture of the Central Plains. "Three Visits to Zhuge Liang's Thatched Cottage" and "The Old Steed over the Manger" are two classical stories that took place against the background of the great division in the Wei, Jin, and Southern and Northern dynasties. Both Liu Bei and Cao Cao had ambitions to unify the world, and the spirit of courtesy and courage embodied in the stories is still loved by people today.

第三章

隋唐典故

Chapter 3

Allusions in Sui and Tang Dynasties

隋唐时期是指从公元581年隋朝建立，到907年唐朝灭亡的这段时期，是中国历史上最强盛的时期之一，是经历了五胡乱华和南北朝两个漫长分裂动荡时期后的大一统王朝。隋唐时期在政治、军事、文化、经济、科技上都达到了前所未有的发展高度。河南是当时政治演变、经济文化发展的重要舞台，东都的营造、大运河的开通使洛阳成为交通中心，洛阳同时也是当时国际化的大都市。

一、营造东都

洛阳有着5000多年文明史、4000多年城市史、1500多年建都史。洛阳是华夏文明的发祥地之一、丝绸之路的东方起点、隋唐大运河的中心，历史上先后有十三个王朝在洛阳建都。隋唐时期，洛阳得到了极大的发展，并在唐睿宗年间被武则天改称为"神都"，她称帝之后更是将"神都"作为武周的都城，直到21年后"神都"又被改为"东京"，是中国历史上唯一被命名为"神都"的城市。"神都"是一个充满神奇色彩的城市，那么这个城市在隋唐时期又是何时开始修建的呢？

公元581年，隋文帝杨坚夺取北周政权建立隋朝，并以长安为首都。此时的长安作为隋朝的都城可谓是盛极一时。但是长安也有它的缺点，地处西北，难以控制广大的中原和南方地区，再有，长安的水路、陆路交通不便，且周围没有富饶的粮食种植地，经常出现饥荒情况，这使得隋炀帝不得不另选一个都城来代替长安成为新的首都。

公元604年，隋炀帝巡视洛阳，在北登邙岭、南望伊阙时发出感叹："这难道不是龙门吗？自古以来人们为什么不把都城设在这里？"一旁的苏威赶紧回答道："自古以来人们并非不知道这里，只是在等待陛下罢了。"隋炀帝听了之后非常高兴。在综合考虑洛阳的情况之后，公元605年，隋炀帝下令，命尚书令杨素为营造大监，杨达、宇文恺为副监，在邙山以南、伊阙之北、涧水以东、瀍河两侧新建东都。在营建东都的

The period of Sui and Tang dynasties, one of the most prosperous periods in Chinese history, started with the establishment of Sui in 581 AD and ended with the fall of Tang in 907 AD. It is a grand unification after two periods of division and turbulence, namely the period of five nomadic peoples invading the Central Plains and the Southern and Northern dynasties. The Sui and Tang period witnessed the unprecedented development of politics, military strength, culture, economics and science and technology. Henan was an important stage for political evolution and economic and cultural development at that time, and the construction of the Eastern Capital and the opening of the Grand Canal made Luoyang a transportation center and an international metropolis.

I. Building the Eastern Capital

Luoyang has more than 5,000 years of history of civilization, more than 4,000 years of urban history and more than 1,500 years of capital construction history. It is one of the birthplaces of Chinese culture, the eastern starting point of the Silk Road, the centre of the Sui and Tang Canal, and the capital of 13 dynasties. During the Sui and Tang period, Luoyang developed greatly and was renamed the "Capital of Gods" by Wu Zetian in the years of Emperor Ruizong of Tang. After she became the empress, she made the "Capital of Gods" the capital of Wu Zhou. Twenty-one years later, the name "Capital of Gods" was changed to "Eastern Capital". But Luoyang is the only city in Chinese history that had the name "Capital of Gods". It was a city full of magical colors. So, you may wonder when the construction of the city began in the Sui and Tang period.

In 581 AD, Yang Jian, Emperor Wen of Sui, seized power from the Northern Zhou and established the Sui Dynasty with Chang'an as its capital which was in its prime then. But Chang'an also had its drawbacks. Located in the northwest, it was difficult to control the vast areas of the Central Plains and the south. Moreover, Chang'an had poor water and land transportation, and there was no abundant food growing areas around it. Frequent famines forced Emperor Yang of Sui to choose another city to replace Chang'an as the new capital.

In 604 AD, Emperor Yang inspected Luoyang. When gazing at Yi Que in the south on top of Ridge Mang in the north, Emperor Yang exclaimed, "Is this

营造东都
Building the Eastern Capital

时候，由于从江南运输物资不便，河北物资丰富但不便管理，于是隋炀帝在营造东都的同时开凿运河。运河分为四段，分别为济渠、永济渠、江南河、广通渠。运河的开通使得洛阳可以北接河北、南通江南，将南北物资都汇聚洛阳，洛阳也因此快速建设起来。

营造东都花费了整整一年时间，即从大业元年（公元605年）三月到二年（公元606年）正月。此时的隋炀帝正在江南巡游，听说东都建成，立刻带着六宫、百官及眷属等大批人于当年四月抵达洛阳，并命令洛阳周边的百姓以及各地的富商大贾搬进东都居住。

新建的东都极其壮观华丽。东都的建设仿照长安，分为宫城、皇城以及外郭城三部分。城郭周围达27千米，城西为100千米的上林苑，

not Dragon Gate? Why has no one ever thought of building the capital here?" Su Wei quickly replied, "It's not that this place has not been known for a long time; it has just been waiting for Your Majesty." Emperor Yang was very glad at that and in 605 AD, after making a comprehensive survey of Luoyang, he appointed Yang Su, the Secretary of the State, as the chief inspector and Yang Da and Yuwen Kai as the deputy supervisors to be responsible for the building of the capital within the boundary of Ridge Mang in the north, Yi Que in the south, Jian River in the west and along the banks of Chan River. Meanwhile Emperor Yang also embarked on the project of digging a canal in order to transport the materials from the south of the Yangtze River and manage the sufficient supplies beyond the north of the Yellow River. The canal was divided into four sections: Ji Canal, Yongji Canal, Jiangnan River, and Guangtong Canal. The canal connected Luoyang to the Yellow River in the north and the Yangtze River in the south, bringing supplies from both the north and the south regions to Luoyang so that the capital could be rapidly built.

From the third month of 605 AD, the first year of Daye, to the first month of 606 AD, it took a whole year to build the Eastern Capital. At this time, Emperor Yang was touring the south of the Yangtze River. At the news of its completion, he immediately went to Luoyang and arrived in the fourth month with his wives and concubines, together with his officials and their families. Meanwhile, he ordered the people around Luoyang and wealthy merchants from all over the country to move into the Eastern Capital.

The newly built capital was extremely spectacular and gorgeous. The construction was modeled after Chang'an, and the area was divided into three parts: the capital city, the imperial city and the rampart. It was 27 kilometers along the city wall, and in the west was the imperial park of Shanglin, consisting of 16 courtyards. Near the city was located a pool which exceeded 5 kilometers in size, and a large number of granaries were set up around the city beside the canal, including the Liyang Warehouse and the Heyang Warehouse. Within the capital city, the Ziluo Warehouse was built for storing grain and salt. In addition, two warehouses were built near Taihe Gate, presumably for storing grain and cloth. Hanjia Granary was built for the same purpose in the north. The capital also had three large markets: Datong Market in the south, Tongyuan Market in the north,

内设 16 院。近城处更是有超过 5 千米的凝碧池，城周围及运河旁设置了大量的粮仓，如黎阳仓、河阳仓等。宫城内部还设置子罗仓来储存盐粮。除此之外，宫城泰和门有两间藏库，东城北部还有 47 万平方米的含嘉仓城，据推测这两处是用来储藏粮食和布匹的。东都城内还设有三处商业市场，分别是南市大同市、北市通远市、东市丰都市。其中，通远市在漕渠边上，为水路市集，聚集各地来京的数万货物的船舶；丰都市则规模最大，里面有许多店铺，其中仅仅是市集四面外围的店铺就有四百余家，货物云集，人声鼎沸，热闹非凡。这三处市场不仅是当时中国的交易中心，更是对外的贸易场所。隋炀帝曾下令整顿市场，市场内部店铺十分整齐划一，设置了许多帷帐，装满了奇珍异宝，胡人胡商经过可直接坐下吃饭喝酒，且店家会以中国丰饶为由，不收取他们的饭钱和酒钱，以此向他们展示中国的强盛。这虽然体现了隋炀帝的奢侈铺张，但也从侧面体现了当时洛阳的繁华景象。

自古以来，有许多人对隋朝灭亡的原因进行讨论，营造东都就是其中的一个重大原因。据史书记载，营造东都征役八十万，除此之外，还征了十多万的木工、瓦工、金工、石工等。建设的过程更是耗费了极大的人力、物力。民工首先需要前往江南地区砍大树，一棵大树就需要两千人进行拖行，东都与江南之间相隔千里，民工将其送至东都后再返回，因为东都建设急迫，累死的、饿死的、被小吏奴役死的民工大约占总数的一半。除了营建东都外，隋炀帝开凿大运河、三征高句丽等活动都大量地消耗了国力，最终使得民怨沸腾，群雄并起，隋朝仅存三十余年便灭亡。

隋朝覆灭后，李唐王朝建立，仍以长安作为都城。唐太宗改洛阳为洛阳宫，贞观年间多次修缮东都。唐太宗曾先后四次来洛阳处理国政，在洛阳居住了两年之久。唐高宗将洛阳改为东都，并频频往来于东西都之间，而且居住东都的时间更长，在永淳元年（公元 682 年）关内饥荒之时，更是废西京长安，迁往洛阳，之后再未回长安。高宗驾崩，武则

and Fengdu Market in the east. Among these, Tongyuan was a waterway market built on the bank of Cao Canal, gathering tens of thousands of cargo ships from all over the country. Fengdu Market was the largest in scale, holding more than 400 shops scattered on the outskirts of the market, abounding in goods and noisy with people coming and going. These three markets were centers for both domestic and foreign trade. Emperor Yang once ordered the market to be restored, and the shops inside the market were made very neat and uniform, with many draperies and treasures. The Hu people and Hu merchants could sit down directly to eat and drink. The shopkeepers would not charge them for food and wine in order to show them the abundance and strength of China. It was a reflection of Emperor Yang's extravagance as well as Luoyang's prosperity at that time.

Historians have long discussed the reasons why the Sui Dynasty perished quickly and it's believed that the building of the Eastern Capital was one of the major reasons. According to historical records, 800,000 people were conscripted to build the Eastern Capital, and in addition, more than 100,000 carpenters, bricklayers, metal workers, and stone workers were also recruited. The building of the capital required substantial manpower and material resources. First of all, the laborers had to go to the south of Yangtze River to cut down trees and it took 2000 people to move by hand a thick tree trunk to Luoyang a thousand miles away and then the laborers had to return immediately to the south for more lumber. In the process of building the capital, half of the laborers died from fatigue, hunger, and maltreatment by minor officers. In addition to building the capital, the digging of the canal and three expeditions to Koguryo (Korea) were also exhausting tasks which kindled people's resentment toward the government and accelerated the collapse of Sui which existed for only over thirty years.

After the fall of the Sui Dynasty, the Tang Dynasty of Li's clan was established, still with Chang'an as its capital. Emperor Taizong turned Luoyang into Luoyang Palace and renovated the Eastern Capital several times during the Zhenguan years. Emperor Taizong came to Luoyang four times to handle state affairs and lived there for two years. Emperor Gaozong converted Luoyang into the Eastern Capital and frequently came and went between Luoyang and Chang'an, staying longer in Luoyang. In 682 AD, the first year of Yongchun, a famine broke out and Emperor Gaozong moved the capital to Luoyang and

天操控政局，后改国号为"周"，登基为帝，将洛阳作为都城，并称之为"神都"。中宗迁居长安，玄宗又将都城迁回洛阳。安史之乱后，洛阳在战火中衰落下来，一直持续到宋代的建立。但从宋代开始一直到新中国的建立，洛阳再未成为统一王朝的都城。随着近些年洛阳的旅游业和文化产业快速发展，洛阳对一些古建筑也进行了维修和保护，千年都城的风采逐渐展现在世人面前，人们也终将见识到美丽繁华的新时代洛阳焕发出新的光彩！

never returned to Chang'an during his reign. After Emperor Gaozong died, Wu Zetian controlled the political situation, changed the name of the country to "Zhou", ascended to the throne as the empress, and made Luoyang the capital, calling it the "Capital of Gods". Emperor Zhongzong moved to Chang'an and Emperor Xuanzong moved back to Luoyang. After the event of An Lushan's Rebellion, Luoyang began to decline until the Song Dynasty was founded. But from the Song Dynasty till the founding of the People's Republic of China, Luoyang never again becomes the capital of a unified dynasty. With the rapid development of Luoyang's tourism and cultural industry in recent years, Luoyang has also renovated and protected some ancient buildings, and the glamor of the millennium capital city has gradually been displayed in front of the world, and people will eventually see the beautiful and prosperous Luoyang in the new era glowing with new brilliance!

二、僧救唐王

"僧救唐王"是少林寺发展历史中一个重要的事件,同时它也是唐王朝建立过程中的一个具有重要意义的转折点。"僧救唐王"不仅使得唐王朝最终完成了统一大业,同时也使得少林寺名声大振。

对于"僧救唐王"这件历史事件,少林寺至今仍保存着许多的史料记载。在少林寺的大雄宝殿前面,有一块名为"太宗文皇帝圣旨碑"的石碑,上面清楚地记载着李世民登基后对少林寺僧的封赐以及参与事件的十三棍僧的法名。除此之外,少林寺的白衣殿后壁上还画着在古洛阳城东门外,十三棍僧一边抵御追兵,一边保护李世民的场景。这些史料生动地再现了当时的情景。

僧救唐王
Shaolin Monks Rescuing the King of Tang

"僧救唐王"发生在隋末唐初时期。隋朝因隋炀帝好大喜功、劳民伤财而亡,天下群雄并起、逐鹿中原。此时的社会战争频仍、动荡不安。少林寺作为佛教寺庙也难逃战乱的影响。隋炀帝在位期间大力推崇佛教,曾将位于少林寺西北25千米的柏谷坞100顷良田赐给少林寺作为供养

II. Shaolin Monks Rescuing the King of Tang

"Shaolin Monks Rescuing the King of Tang" was an important event in the history of Shaolin Temple, and it was also a significant turning point in the process of the establishment of the Tang Dynasty. The righteous act of the monks rescuing the king not only allowed the Tang Dynasty to complete the great cause of unification, but also helped Shaolin Temple win great fame.

Many records of the historical event of "Shaolin Monks Rescuing the King of Tang" are still preserved at Shaolin Temple. In front of the Grand Hall of Shaolin Temple, there is a stone stele called "Monument to the Imperial Edict of Emperor Taizong", which clearly records the names of the thirteen stick-wielding monks who participated in the event and how Li Shimin awarded them after he ascended to the throne. Moreover, on the back wall of the White Palace of the temple, there is a drawing of the 13 monks resisting the soldiers in defense of Li Shimin outside the eastern gate of Luoyang.

This event happened in the period of the late Sui and early Tang. The Sui Dynasty was then dying due to Emperor Yang's love of fame and extravagance. The society at that time was unstable with peasant uprisings everywhere and Shaolin Temple was also affected by the social turbulence. When Emperor Yang was in power, he esteemed Buddhism and gave Shaolin Temple more than 1600 acres of fertile land at the village of Baiguwu, 25 kilometers to the northwest of Shaolin Temple. Since then, Shaolin Temple had become a large temple with more than 1600 acres of fertile land. After obtaining this land, Shaolin Temple arranged for some monks to use it and take care of it, which greatly increased the income of the temple. But at the end of the Sui Dynasty, Shaolin Temple, which had a lot of land and grain, was attacked by the peasant army, and in a tragic event, the peasant army burned down the temple, leaving only a solitary tower. In this case, the temple had to organize martial monks to protect its own field property and three of the 13 stick-wielding monks, including Tanzong, were responsible for this task. Later on, when Wang Shichong occupied Luoyang, he sent his nephew Wang Renze to Baiguwu to build a military stronghold to protect Luoyong. The property of Shaolin Temple was seized without any compensation, which irritated

寺院的田产。自此，少林寺成为拥有万亩良田的大寺院。在得了这处田产后，少林寺便安排一些僧人前去种植、打理，为寺庙增加了不少的收入。但到了隋末，拥有众多田产粮食的少林寺受到了农民军的攻击，并发生了农民军将少林寺烧得仅剩一座孤塔的惨案。在这种情况下，少林寺不得不组织武僧来保护自己的田产，十三棍僧中的昙宗等三人担任着保护田产的职责。后来王世充占领洛阳后，为保护洛阳安全，派自己的侄子王仁则去柏谷坞建立军事重镇来拱卫洛阳。这使得少林寺的田产受到侵占，少林寺在田产被占后并未收到任何的补偿，这激怒了少林寺众僧，而少林寺众僧虽然武艺高强但寡不敌众，难以同王世充的军队正面对抗，于是他们按下了心中的愤恨，准备寻求机会赶走王世充，夺回田产。

此时的李世民作为唐高祖李渊的儿子，正在为刚成立不久还未统一全国的唐王朝东奔西走，打败割据势力，扩大唐王朝的统治版图。在李世民平定了山西的宋金刚和刘武周之后，天下的割据势力就只剩下了中原的王世充和华北的窦建德。王世充是原隋的大将，盘踞在洛阳，号称郑国皇帝，拥有大量的兵马。窦建德号称夏国皇帝，也在积极地招兵买马，扩大地盘，这二人是唐统一天下最大的阻碍。公元585年，李世民率领唐军进攻洛阳，但洛阳防守甚为严密，唐军四面攻城，昼夜不息，半个多月后也未见任何成果。此时的唐军疲惫不堪，士气低下，希望能够撤军回朝，就连唐军总管刘弘基等也请求李世民停止围攻洛阳，但在李世民的强烈坚持下，唐军继续攻打洛阳。王世充在唐军攻洛前已经致信窦建德请求兵力援助。窦建德害怕王世充被杀之后下一个唐军攻击的目标就是自己，出于唇亡齿寒的考虑，率领对外宣称三十万大军实则只有十万余人的军队渡过黄河，攻陷荥阳、阳翟等地，之后准备西进洛阳，和王世充里应外合夹击李世民。

面对这种危机，李世民在和部下讨论之后让李元吉留守继续攻打洛阳，自己则带三千多精兵赶赴西边阻止窦建德前进，防止王、窦二人联合起来。在李世民走后，李元吉被王世充所派的大将杨公卿、单雄信所

the monks of the temple. Though the monks were strong in martial arts, they were outnumbered and could not confront Wang Shichong's army face to face, so they decided to look for opportunities to drive away Wang's army and win back their property.

Li Shimin, son of Li Yuan, the first emperor of Tang, was fighting in both the east and the west for the young Tang Dynasty to defeat separatist forces and expand the Tang's ruling territory. After Song Jingang and Liu Wuzhou in Shanxi were pacified, only the forces of Wang Shichong in the Central Plains and Dou Jiande in the north remained. Wang Shichong was a general of the Sui Dynasty. He lived in Luoyang and was known as the king of Zheng. He had a large number of soldiers and horses. Dou Jiande, known as the king of Xia, was also actively recruiting soldiers and expanding his territory, and these two men were the biggest obstacles to the unification of the Tang Dynasty. In 585 AD, Li Shimin led the Tang army to attack Luoyang from all sides unceasingly, but the battle lasted for over two weeks without any success since the defense was very tight. Tired and demoralized, the Tang's soldiers asked to retreat, and even Liu Hongji the commander pleaded with Li Shimin to stop besieging Luoyang. Under Li Shimin's insistence, the attack continued. In fact, before the Tang's army attacked Luoyang, Wang Shichong had asked Dou Jiande for additional troops, and out of the consideration of his own safety, Dou agreed because if Wang was defeated, Dou believed Li Shimin's next goal would be Dou himself. Then, leading an army of over 100,000 soldiers, claimed to be 300,000, Dou crossed the Yellow River and conquered Xingyang and Yangzhai, ready to march west toward Luoyang and join Wang Shichong to confront Li Shimin together.

Facing this crisis, Li Shimin discussed with his subordinates and asked Li Yuanji to stay and continue the fight while he himself would rush westward with over 3000 well-trained soldiers to stop Dou Jiande from advancing to unite with Wang Shichong. After Li Shimin left, Li Yuanji was defeated by Wang Shichong's generals Yang Gongqing and Shan Xiongxin, and Lu Yin'e, the head of the army, was also killed in the battle. Meanwhile, Li Shimin also had difficulty resisting Dou's strong army, thus the Tang army was threatened on both sides and fell into an extremely dangerous situation. At this news, the monks of Shaolin Temple, filled with resentment towards Wang Renze, decided to help Li Shimin

打败，行军总管卢尹谔也在战斗中丧命。李世民难以抵挡窦建德的十万大军，唐军两面都受到威胁，陷入了极其危险的境地。此时的少林寺众僧满怀对王仁则的愤恨，在听说李世民陷入险境之后，准备助李世民一臂之力早日结束战争，在善护、志操、惠玚、昙宗的带领下，少林寺众僧经过慎重考虑，层层筛选出十三人，之后展开了营救唐军的行动。是夜，十三棍僧一举攻入王仁则大营，在经过几番激烈的斗争后，活捉了王仁则，并将其献给唐军，王仁则所在的州城随之土崩瓦解。至此唐军的一大威胁被解除。

李世民在被十三棍僧救助回归唐军后即刻派人将他亲手写的嘉奖信送往少林寺，信中高度赞扬了十三棍僧擒获王仁则，帮助唐军打败王世充的义举。据《少林寺牒》记载，李世民不仅对十三棍僧进行了赞扬，还准备给他们一些官职。但僧人们拒绝了实质性官职，于是李世民只好封少林寺参战十三武僧以勋位——"上座僧善护、寺主僧志操、都维那僧惠玚、大将军僧昙宗、同立功僧普惠、明嵩、灵宪、普胜、智守、道广、智光、满、丰"，后来又赏赐千段丝绸。又过了几年，李世民特赐少林寺良田四十顷、水碾一具。

十三棍僧的仗义相救是李世民攻打王世充一役中不可或缺的转折点，对这一战役的胜利起到了极为重要的作用。正是十三棍僧的及时出手，使得李世民和唐军能够转危为安继而打败窦建德，迫使王世充投降，最终帮助唐高祖完成统一大业。

对于十三棍僧的义举，李世民评价颇高，更是在贞观年间颁行的《少林寺牒》中将这一战中少林寺十三武僧助唐擒获王仁则的功劳，同唐军在武牢关战胜窦建德的功劳画等号，可见其重要性。这一战役不仅是李世民生平中为数不多的重要战役，同时也是对唐王朝顺利统一全国起决定性作用的重要战役。经此一役，唐军彻底铲除了所有割据势力，统一全国，为后来的大唐盛世奠定了基础。

to end the war as soon as possible. Under the leadership of Shanhu, Zhicao, Huiyang, and Tanzong, 13 monks of Shaolin Temple were screened out after a careful consideration, and then they launched an operation to rescue the Tang army. That night, those 13 stick-wielding monks stormed into Wang Renze's camp. After several fierce battles, they captured Wang alive and turned him over to the Tang army. Wang Renze's town collapsed and one of Tang's threats was removed.

Immediately after the capture of Wang Renze, Li Shimin was rescued by the monks. He wrote a letter of commendation and sent it to Shaolin Temple. In the letter, he highly praised those 13 monks for capturing Wang Renze and helping the Tang army defeat Wang Shichong. According to *The Documents of Shaolin Temple*, Li Shimin not only praised the monks, but was prepared to give them some official positions. The monks rejected the offer and then Li Shimin could do nothing but grant them each a noble title. The group included the eminent monk Shanhu, the temple's chief monk Zhicao, the Duweina Monk Huiyang, the Great General Monk Tanzong, and the fellow meritorious monks including Puhui, Mingsong, Lingxian, Pusheng, Zhishou, Daoguang, Zhiguang, Mann, and Feng. Later on, Li Shimin also rewarded them with a thousand pieces of silk. A few more years, Li Shimin specially gave Shaolin Temple more than 600 acres of fertile land and a set of water grinds.

The rescue by the 13 monks was a turning point in Li Shimin's attack on Wang Shichong, and played a vital role in Li's victory in the battle. It was the timely action of the thirteen monks that enabled Li Shimin to defeat Dou Jiande, force Wang Shichong to surrender, and ultimately help Emperor Gaozu of Tang complete the cause of unification.

Li Shimin thought very highly of the righteous act of the 13 monks. *The Documents of Shaolin Temple*, issued in the Zhenguan period, associated this act with the victory of Tang's army over Dou Jiande at Wulao Pass to manifest its significance. This battle was not only one of the few important battles in Li Shimin's life, but also a significant one that decided whether the Tang Dynasty could smoothly unify the whole country. After this battle, the Tang army completely eliminated all the separatist forces and finished the process of unification, laying the foundation for the ensuing heyday of the Tang Dynasty.

三、玄奘取经

玄奘取经
Xuanzang Going to the West for the Buddhist Sutras

玄奘（公元602年—公元664年），俗姓陈，名祎，洛阳缑氏人（今河南偃师缑氏镇），十三岁出家，玄奘是其法名，后人称他三藏法师（三藏是对佛教经典的三个部分——佛经、戒律、论述与注解的总称，通晓三藏的僧人被称为三藏法师）。

唐初，玄奘在四川、长安等地研究佛教理论，感到佛教分成许多宗派，佛经译文多误，自己无所适从，想亲自到天竺（印度的古称）学佛

III. Xuanzang Going to the West for the Buddhist Sutras

Xuanzang (602 AD-664 AD), with Chen Yi being his secular name, was born out of the clan of Gouzhi in Luoyang. He was ordained at the age of 13, and took Xuanzang as his dharma name. He was later known as Sanzang Master (Sanzang is a general term for the three parts of the Buddhist scriptures—Buddhist scriptures, precepts, discourses and annotations, and monks who are familiar with Sanzang are called Sanzang Masters).

In the early Tang Dynasty, Xuanzang went to many places such as Sichuan and Chang'an to study Buddhist theories. Confused about the fact that Buddhism was divided into many schools and there were many mistakes in the translation of the scriptures available to him, he decided to go to Tenjiku (Ancient India) to study the sutras and do research on the problematic issues of Buddhist teachings. He planned to travel to the west from Chang'an with several companions, who were reluctant because the Turkic people were disturbing the borders and private departures were prohibited temporarily.

In 627 AD, the first year of Zhenguan (also said to be the second or third year), Xuanzang set out from Chang'an, mingling with merchants returning to the Western Regions. He snuck over Yumen Pass and went west on his own. At the end of the summer of 628 AD, he arrived in the northwest of Tenjiku. Along the route from west to east, he visited the pagoda with a height of over 100 meters built for Shakyamuni Buddha by Worry-free King. Other relics he visited included the birthplace and the deathplace of Buddha and the synagogue where he taught the scriptures. In Nabudi (present-day Punjab Province, India), Xuanzang investigated the legend about how Chinese peaches and pears were introduced into India. Four years later, in the fourth year of Zhenguan (630 AD), he arrived in Magadha (present-day south of Bihar of India) and went to Nalanda Monastery, the foremost educational institution of Tenjiku Buddhism. Jie Xian, the presiding monk, was then the authority on Buddhism of India. When Xuanzang arrived, he was warmly welcomed, and more than a thousand people held incense and flowers along the road to greet him. Jie Xian was then over a hundred years old, and he no longer lectured, but in order to show his

经，研究解决关于佛教教义的一些疑难问题。他在长安结伴准备出国西游，由于唐朝初建，突厥贵族扰边，暂时禁止私人出境，同伴退缩。

贞观元年（公元627年，另有贞观二年、三年说），他从长安出发，杂于返西域的客商中，偷越玉门关，然后独自西行，于公元628年夏末，到达天竺西北部，然后沿一条由西向东的路线访问参谒了古代无忧王为释迦牟尼佛建造的一百多米高的佛塔以及佛诞生处、逝世处、说法的讲堂等胜迹，还在至那仆底国（今印度旁遮普省）调查了有关中国的桃、梨传进印度的传说，这样度过了四年。贞观四年（公元630年），他到达摩揭陀国（今印度比哈尔邦南部），来到那烂陀寺。那烂陀寺是天竺佛教的最高学府。该寺主持（当家和尚）戒贤是当时印度的佛学权威。玄奘到达时受到热烈欢迎，一千多人捧香、花沿路迎接，时戒贤已一百多岁，本已不再讲学，但为表示对中国的友好情谊，特意收玄奘为弟子，用十五个月的时间给他讲了最难懂的佛经——《瑜珈论》。玄奘用了整整五年时间精研佛学理论，并研究了波罗门教经典、印度方言，取得优异成绩。全寺除戒贤通晓全部理论外，能通晓二十部的有一千人，通晓三十部的有五百人，通晓五十部的只有十人，即十大法师，玄奘即其中之一。但他并未满足于此，公元636年，辞戒贤外出游学，一路上多次参加各地的辩论会，战胜许多学者，声誉满天竺。

公元640年，玄奘返回那烂陀寺，戒贤叫他主持寺内讲座。戒贤有一位弟子，对经论不能贯通，玄奘用梵文（古印度文）写了一篇论文，阐发义理，指明其谬误，得戒贤与僧众同声赞誉。那时曷利沙帝国已统一了天竺北部，国君戒日王崇信佛教，本人又是诗人、剧作家，经他提倡的各宗教学派论辩争鸣十分活跃。有一个反对那烂陀派的人写了一篇论文呈给戒日王，声称无人能驳倒一个字。戒日王把论文转给戒贤，并决定在国都曲女城（今印度北方邦卡瑙季）举行学术大会公开辩论。戒日王非常高兴地会见玄奘，玄奘介绍了中国的政治、经济、文化、艺术

friendship with China, he specially accepted Xuanzang as a disciple and spent fifteen months teaching him the most difficult Buddhist scripture—*Yoga Theory*. Xuanzang devoted five years of his life to the study of Buddhist theory, and excelled in the classics of the Brahmin religion and the Indian dialect. In addition to the abbot who knew all the theories, there were 1,000 people who knew 20 theories, 500 people who knew 30 theories, and only 10 people who knew 50 theories. Xuanzang was one of them. But he was not satisfied with this. In 636 AD, he bade farewell to Jie Xian and went out on a study trip. Along the way, he participated in many debates in various places, defeating many scholars and gaining tremendous fame in Tenjiku.

In 640 AD, Xuanzang returned to Nalanda Monastery, and Jie Xian asked him to preside over the lectures in the temple. Since one of the disciples of Jie Xian could not understand the scriptures, Xuanzang wrote a treatise in Sanskrit (Ancient Indian) to expound the doctrine and point out its errors, and was praised by the monks in unison. By that time, the north of Tenjiku had been united by the Horisha Empire and Jie Ri, the king, was a Buddhist. Also as a poet and playwright, he was active in upholding religious disputes and contentions. One of the opponents of the Nalanda sect wrote a paper and presented it to King Jie Ri, claiming that no one could refute a single word. Then the king forwarded the paper to Jie Xian and decided to hold an open debate conference in the capital city called Kanyakubja (Kanauj of North India today). King Jie Ri was very pleased to meet with Xuanzang, who introduced to the king Chinese politics, economy, culture and art. Showing great interest in these matters, King Jie Ri expressed his intention to visit China in person.

The debate was held in December of 642 AD, the sixteenth year of Zhenguan, and the participants included kings from the 18 kingdoms of Tenjiku, more than 3000 Buddhists, over 2000 believers in Brahmanism and other sects and over 1000 monks from Nalanda Monastery. As the key speaker, Xuanzang read a paper entitled *On Mastering Evils* in Sanskrit, and having this paper transcribed and hung at the entrance to the conference hall, Xuanzang declared that if anyone could refute a word justifiably, he would have himself beheaded to apologize. Five days passed by and nobody came to debate. The conference went on for 18 days and everyone was impressed by Xuanzang's incisive arguments.

情况，引起戒日王很大兴趣，表示要亲自到中国访问。贞观十六年（公元642年）十二月，辩论大会开始，与会者有天竺十八国的国王、佛教徒三千多人、婆罗门等教徒两千多人，那烂陀寺来了一千多人。玄奘担任大会的论主（主讲人），他用梵文写了一篇《制恶见论》作为辩论的主题在会上宣读，同时誊写一份悬挂在会场门口，并依照惯例声明："如有人能据理驳倒一个字，就斩下论主的头以谢罪。"可是五天过去了，仍没有人来辩论。大会连续举行十八天，大家都被玄奘的精辟议论所折服。结束那天，戒日王送给他金钱一万、银钱三万，僧衣一百领。十八国王也各以厚礼相赠，他全部谢绝了，最后戒日王恳请玄奘乘坐一头用精美华幢装饰的大象游行一周，又特邀他参加七十五天的无遮大会（五年一次的天竺佛教盛会），表达对这位中国大师的尊敬。

公元643年，深切怀念祖国的玄奘表示将要回国，戒日王一再挽留他，甚至表示只要玄奘肯留下，愿为他建造一百所寺院，但他归志已定，戒日王只好答应。朋友们争相赠礼，玄奘一一谢绝，只接受了鸠摩罗国王送的一件鹿毛披肩，以备途中防雨。动身那天，戒日王、鸠摩罗国王等以及当地人民送他几十里路才洒泪而别。

公元645年正月二十四日，玄奘带着657部佛经，经西域回到长安。唐太宗在洛阳行宫接见他，极有兴趣地听他介绍西域及天竺见闻，并劝他还俗到朝廷任职，他婉言谢绝。三月初一，玄奘回长安，随即开始佛经翻译工作，先后在弘福寺和慈恩寺主持译场，译场有负责翻译的，有检查译意的，有整理译文的，有推敲字句的，各任专职，分工细密。玄奘不懈地工作了19年，共译出佛经75部、1335卷，由于他有较高的汉文化素养又精通梵文，所以他的译文流畅优美，而且忠于原意，有些专用名词如"印度"一词、表示时间的"刹那"一词就是他确定的。唐太宗亲自为玄奘的译经写了《大唐三藏圣教序》，借以宣扬佛教。

玄奘还回忆旅途见闻，由弟子记录，写了一本《大唐西域记》，记载了亲历的110国、传闻的28国的情况，涉及地域包括阿富汗、巴基斯坦、

On the last day of the conference, King Jie Ri gave him 10,000 gold cash, 30,000 silver cash, and 100 pieces of monk cloth as a reward. The eighteen kings also gave Xuanzang generous gifts, but he declined all of them, and finally King Jie Ri asked Xuanzang to ride for a week's parade on an elephant exquisitely decorated, and invited him to participate in a seventy-five-day open-air conference (a Tenjiku Buddhist Festival held every five years) to show his reverence for this Chinese master.

In 643 AD, Xuanzang, who deeply missed his motherland, said he was going to return to China. King Jie Ri kept asking him to stay. He even offered to build a hundred monasteries for Xuanzang as long as Xuanzang was willing to stay. However, Xuanzang made up his mind to return, and the king had no choice but to agree. Friends rushed to present gifts, but Xuanzang declined one by one, accepting only a shawl of deer fur from the king of Gomorrah, in case of rain on the way. On the day of his departure, King Jie Ri, the king of Gomorrah, together with the local people, escorted him for dozens of miles before they said goodbye in tears.

On January 24, 645 AD, Xuanzang returned to Chang'an via the Western Regions with 657 Buddhist scriptures. Emperor Taizong received him in Luoyang, and with great interest he listened to Xuanzang's introduction to what he had seen and heard in Western Regions and Tenjiku. When Emperor Taizong advised him to return to secular life and serve in the imperial court, Xuanzang politely refused. On the first day of March, Xuanzang returned to Chang'an and embarked immediately on the work of the sutra translation, presiding over two sessions of translation at Hongfu Temple and Ci'en Temple one after the other. This undertaking involved translating, checking, sorting, and deliberating, the division of labor being meticulous. Xuanzang worked tirelessly for 19 years, translating 75 Buddhist sutras into 1,335 volumes. Owing to his great learning of Chinese culture and his proficiency in Sanskrit, his translation was smooth and graceful, and faithful to its original meaning. Some proper nouns like "印度" (India) and "刹那" (expressing time like "a splitting second") were decided by him. Emperor Taizong even wrote a preface to his translations, entitled *Preface to the Sacred Teachings of Tang Sanzang* to proclaim Buddhism.

Based on his memories of his travels and transcribed by his pupils, Xuanzang

印度、孟加拉国、尼泊尔、斯里兰卡等国家。他把当时各国的方位、道路、疆域、城市、人口、风俗人情、名胜古迹、历史人物、传说故事等一一写下来,内容丰富生动,准确可靠,是研究这些地区历史的重要材料。现在《大唐西域记》已被译成数国文字,成为一部世界名著。玄奘当时可能认为他留给后世的主要贡献是取回的佛经和他的译经,我们今天看来,他那些宣扬佛教的经书的总和也未必抵得上这一部《大唐西域记》的价值。玄奘也向天竺介绍了中国的文化,据说他曾经把中国道教哲学著作《老子》译成梵文,传入印度,这应是第一部中国典籍的外文译本,但现已散佚。

天竺朋友十分怀念他,高宗永徽三年(公元652年),天竺和尚法长来中国,玄奘老友那烂陀寺的智光和慧天特意托他给玄奘捎来书信、著作和礼物,表示亲切的问候。信中说:"送去白布两匹,表示我们并没有忘记你,路程太远,希望你不要怪带去的东西太少,还是接受吧。如果你需要什么书,我们会抄出来送去的。"玄奘请法长捎去回信,回赠了礼物,并捎去一份他在回国途中丢失需要补抄的书单,在回信中玄奘感谢朋友们的深情厚谊,对戒贤老师逝世表示深切悼念,还报告了自己的译经工作进展情况,这种动人的友谊是中印人民友谊史上的佳话。

玄奘是中印人民友谊的使者,是唐初佛教高僧,是世界著名的伟大旅行家和杰出的古代翻译家。他能在交通条件还极其落后的时代,用了十八年时间跋涉逾两万千米,征服种种意想不到的困难,完成了自己的艰巨使命,一个重要原因是他具有极其顽强的性格,目标一经确定,就决不动摇,就要以百折不挠的毅力去实现它,这种性格是十分可贵的,他的顽强精神和动人事迹将永远留在中印两国人民的记忆中。

高宗麟德元年(公元664年,《旧唐书》本传作显庆六年,即公元661年),玄奘圆寂于长安附近的玉华寺,葬于长安兴教寺。生平事迹

wrote a book named *Great Tang Records of the Western Regions* which was a record of his first-hand experience of 110 countries directly and that of 28 countries by hearsay. It covered Afghanistan, Pakistan, India, Bangladesh, Nepal, Sri Lanka and other countries. Xuanzang wrote down the locations, roads, territories, cities, populations, customs, places of interest, historical figures, legends and stories of various countries at that time. The contents were rich and vivid, accurate and reliable, offering an important document for the study of the history of these areas. Now this book has been translated into numerous languages and is a renowned masterpiece. Xuanzang may have thought that his main legacy was the sutras he had fetched and his translations, but for us today, the sum of the Buddhist scriptures may not be worth the significance of the book *Great Tang Records of the Western Regions*. Xuanzang also introduced the Chinese culture into Tenjiku, for he was said to have translated *Laozi* into Sanskrit and brought it to India, the first foreign translation of a Chinese classic, which is now lost.

His friends in Tenjiku missed Xuanzang very much. In the third year of Yonghui, Emperor Gao (652 AD), monk Fachang of Tenjiku came to China, and Xuanzang's friends Zhiguang and Huitian from Nalanda Monastery specially entrusted him to bring letters, writings and gifts to Xuanzang as cordial greetings. The letter said, "Here are two pieces of white cloth to show that we miss you. The distance is too far, so we pray you accept them and will not blame on us for bringing too few things. If you need any books, we'll copy them out and send them to you." Xuanzang asked Fachang to take back a letter, a gift, and a list of books that he had lost on his way home. In his reply, Xuanzang thanked his friends for their great kindness, expressed his deep sorrow on Jie Xian's death, and reported the progress of his translation work. This friendship is a touching story in the history of friendship between the Chinese and the Indian peoples.

Xuanzang was a messenger of friendship between the Chinese and the Indian peoples, an eminent Buddhist monk in the early Tang Dynasty, a world-famous great traveler and an outstanding ancient translator. He traveled more than 20,000 kilometers in 18 years when traffic conditions were still extremely backward, conquering all kinds of unexpected difficulties and accomplishing his arduous mission. Behind this was his tenacious character. Once a goal was set, he never wavered, and he achieved it with indomitable perseverance. This character

由其弟子慧立、彦宗撰《大慈恩寺三藏法师传》。唐中叶已有关于玄奘的传说，宋代出现《大唐三藏取经诗话》，明代又有《西游记》，使唐僧成为家喻户晓的人物。

was very precious, and his indomitable spirit and engaging deeds will always be remembered by the peoples of China and India.

In 664 AD, the first year of Linde (in 661 AD, the sixth year of Xianqing, according to *Old Book of Tang*), Emperor Gao, Xuanzang passed away at Yuhua Temple near Chang'an and was buried at Xingjiao Temple in Chang'an. His life deeds were recorded by his disciples Huili and Yanzong in *The Biography of Master Sanzang of the Great Ci'en Temple*. In the middle of the Tang Dynasty, there were already legends about Xuanzang. In the Song Dynasty, a book entitled *A Record of Sanzang Fetching Sutras* appeared. The Ming Dynasty novel *Journey to the West* made Xuanzang a household name.

四、封禅嵩山

武则天是中国历史上唯一的女皇帝,她曾八次驾临嵩山。公元 695 年,她封禅嵩山时,改嵩阳县为登封县。登封作为县级行政单位,从唐朝一直沿用至 20 世纪末期,历时约 1300 年。登封的名称、建制和历史沿革与武则天封禅嵩山有着密不可分的关系。

封禅嵩山

Feng and Shan: Offering Sacrifices on Mount Song

IV. Feng and Shan: Offering Sacrifices on Mount Song

Wu Zetian, the only empress in Chinese history, visited Mount Song eight times. In 695 AD, she changed the name Songyang County into Dengfeng County when she offered sacrifices on Mount Song. As a county-level administrative unit, the name Dengfeng was used from the Tang Dynasty until the end of the 20th century, which lasted for about 1300 years. The name, institutional arrangements and historical development of Dengfeng are closely related to Wu Zetian's practice of worship on Mount Song.

Initially Dengfeng did not appear as a place name. Its original meaning was "climbing the mountain to offer sacrifices". This was an activity undertaken by ancient emperors to worship the heaven and the earth at Eastern Mountain, namely Mount Tai. "On Sacrifice" of the *Shiji* says, "To build an earth altar on Mount Tai to worship the heaven is called Feng. To worship the earth on a lower hill is called Shan." Mount Tai is the most important of the Five Mountains. It is situated in the east and regarded by ancient Chinese people as the best place for the dialogue between the heaven and man. According to a legend, in the ancient times before the Qin Dynasty, "There were 72 emperors who worshiped the heaven on Mount Tai and worshiped the earth on Mount Liangfu." Since the Qin and Han dynasties, many emperors in the historical records have offered sacrifices, including the First Emperor of Qin, Emperor Wu of Han, Emperor Guangwu of Eastern Han, Emperor Gao of Tang, Emperor Xuan of Tang, Emperor Zhen of Song, etc. Empress Wu Zetian is also one of them.

Although Wu Zetian established the Wuzhou regime, she was not called Emperor historically, but Empress Zetian. When Wu Zetian came to the throne, it was clear that the clan of Wu had usurped the world of Li, and that "Changing Tang to Zhou" was a clear sign of the change of the dynasty. The establishment of the Wuzhou Dynasty, although not experiencing a long period of wars like other dynasties, was not smooth. In the years of fierce political fights, many royal nobles and dignitaries were killed because they were dissatisfied with Wu Zetian's dictatorship, and the Wuzhou Dynasty also underwent bloody storms in the process of its establishment. Therefore, offering sacrifices on Mount Song was a

"登封"最初并不是作为地名出现的，其本义是"登山封禅"，是古代帝王在东岳泰山举行的一种祭祀天地活动。《史记·封禅书》云："此泰山上筑土为坛以祭天，报天之功，故曰封。此泰山下小山上除地，报地之功，故曰禅。"泰山为五岳之首，雄踞于东方，被古人看作是天人对话的最佳之地。据传说，在秦朝以前的远古时代，"封泰山禅梁父者七十二家"。秦汉以来，在史籍记载中有多位皇帝举行过封禅大典，如秦始皇、汉武帝、东汉光武帝、唐高宗、唐玄宗、宋真宗等，女皇武则天就是其中的一位。

武则天尽管建立了武周政权，历史上人们却没有把她称为皇帝，而称为则天皇后。武则天做皇帝以后，显然是武姓夺了李姓的天下，"改唐为周"更是改朝换代的明显标志。武周王朝的建立，虽然不像其他王朝那样经历长期征战，但也并非一帆风顺。在多年残酷的政治斗争中，许多皇室贵胄、达官显贵由于对武则天专权不满而被杀，武周王朝在建立的过程中同样也经历血腥风雨。所以，封禅嵩山就是武则天用来宣扬其"丰功伟绩"和"君权神授"的良机，和其他皇帝封禅泰山有异曲同工之妙。那武则天为什么要选择嵩山而不是泰山呢？

这个原因是多方面的。有的学者认为武则天封禅嵩山是从经济方面考虑的，嵩山离洛阳近，花费少，还有一个重要的神秘原因，即中岳之神与武则天同姓"武"姓。其实这并不是武则天选择嵩山作为封禅之地的主要原因。作为一个政治斗争的核心人物，她的一切作为都是以政治目的为中心的。武则天刚临朝称制，徐敬业就以匡复唐室为名于扬州举兵，公开打出了反武旗帜。公元687年，虢州人杨初成也打出了反武旗帜。对这些人的公开反叛，武则天可以派兵镇压。而让武则天头痛的是那些朝中大臣，像裴炎、刘之等人，都是武则天亲自提拔起来的，他们也不满武则天继续把持朝政。武则天非常清楚，她的臣下都受过正统的儒学教育，宁做李唐的旧臣，也不愿做武周的新贵，时刻想着恢复李唐的统治。武则天对公卿大臣并不放心，残酷和恐怖政治只能暂时压制大

good opportunity for Wu Zetian to publicize her "great achievements" and "god-given authority", which had the same effect as other emperors' practice of worship on Mount Tai. Then why did Wu Zetian choose Mount Song instead of Mount Tai?

The reasons for Wu Zetian's choice of Mount Song are manifold. Some scholars believe that her decision was based on economic consideration. Mount Song is close to Luoyang, so it would cost less to travel there. There was also a mysterious reason that matters: the god of Mount Song in central China and Wu Zetian were said to have the same surname "Wu". In fact, this wasn't the main reason why Wu Zetian chose Mount Song as the place of worship. As a central figure in the political struggle, everything she did was centered on political purposes. As soon as Wu Zetian came to power, Xu Jingye raised an army in Yangzhou in the name of restoring the Tang Dynasty, openly opposing Wu. In 687 AD, Yang Chucheng, a native of Guozhou, also rose up against Wu Zetian. As to the open rebellion of these people, Wu Zetian could send troops to suppress it. What caused Wu Zetian a headache was that even those ministers on the court, such as Pei Yan and Liu Zhi, who were promoted by Wu Zetian, were also dissatisfied with her continued reign. Wu Zetian knew very well that her subordinates had received an orthodox Confucian education. She believed they would rather be Li Tang's old vassals than her new upstarts, and thus always thought of restoring the Tang Dynasty. Being at odds with her chancellors, Wu Zetian knew that the politics of cruelty and terror could only temporarily suppress the vassals but not fundamentally solve the problem, therefore she was afraid of leaving Luoyang for Mount Tai.

In September of 684 AD, Wu Zetian changed the name of Luoyang from Eastern Capital to Divine Capital, and Luoyang became the political, economic, cultural, and military center of the Wuzhou Dynasty. Wu Zetian chose Mount Song in the heartland of the Central Plains as the place of worship because, on the one hand, it facilitated her control of the situation since she had won to her favor the time and the place and the support of people; on the other hand, Buddhism and Daoism had played a major role in helping Wu Zetian ascend the throne. In order to appease the chancellors influenced by orthodox Confucian education who opposed her most, Wu Zetian collected a wide range of auspicious

臣，而不能从根本上解决问题，因此她不敢远离洛阳到泰山封禅。

公元684年9月，武则天改东都洛阳为神都，洛阳成为武周王朝的政治、经济、文化、军事中心。中岳嵩山乃是京畿重地，武则天选择嵩山作为封禅之地，一方面便于她控制局势，既占有天时、地利，也不失人和；另一方面，武则天登上帝位，佛教与道教起过重大作用。武则天执掌朝政后，最大的反对派就是那些受过正统儒学教育的朝中显贵。武则天临朝称制之时，广泛收集祥瑞，为自己称帝寻找理论根据，其中佛教起了重要作用。她指使"东魏国寺僧法明等撰《大云经》四卷，表上之，言太后乃弥勒佛下生，当代唐为阎浮提主"，而后又颁《大云经》于天下。在佛教徒极大的吹捧声中，武则天于公元693年9月"加金轮圣神皇帝号"。另外，武则天曾于公元691年4月命令"释教开革命之阶，升于道教之上"。这与她儒、道、佛三家兼容的初衷相违背，不利于她的统治。为了缓和与道教的关系，武则天于公元695年"号嵩山为神岳，尊嵩山神为天中王，夫人为灵妃"。嵩山既有佛教圣地少林寺，又有道家仙观中岳庙，封禅嵩山可以二者兼顾。而且武则天封禅嵩山也可以回避李唐与武周之间的矛盾。按《五经通义》的解释，登山封禅是改朝换代、天下大治的象征。公元666年封禅泰山，李治代表的是李唐王朝，武则天如果再到泰山封禅，代表的将是武周王朝，这意味着武则天篡夺了唐朝的天下，武李矛盾将表面化。武则天与李治是夫妻关系，高宗时代时他们夫妻共同治理天下，再次封禅泰山意味着否定李治，也等于否定自己。在夫权思想占统治地位的封建时代，武则天既不能与李唐王朝公开决裂，也不能把李治当作反面人物，对这种复杂关系，她只能遮遮掩掩。而选择嵩山作为封禅之地，可以巧妙地避开李唐王朝与武周王朝、高宗李治与武则天的关系，回避这些矛盾有利于武则天的统治。

signs and sought a theoretical basis for her claim to the throne, and in this process Buddhism had been of great help. She instructed monk Faming and others from Eastern Wei Temple to compose the four volumes of *The Great Cloud Sutra*, which said that she was the incarnation of Maitreya Buddha, and should be the ruler in the place of the emperor of Tang. Then she promulgated *The Great Cloud Sutra* to the world. To the sounds of vigorous praise of the Buddhists, Wu Zetian was crowned as "Golden Wheel Holy Emperor" in September, 693 AD. In addition, in April of 691 AD, Wu Zetian declared that Buddhism should be esteemed as superior to Daoism owing to its contribution to the establishment of the Wuzhou regime. This ran counter to her original intention of making Confucianism, Daoism, and Buddhism compatible with each other, and was thus not conducive to her rule. In order to ease relations with Daoism, in 695 AD, Wu Zetian "declared Mount Song as sacred, venerating the god of Mount Song as King of Heaven and his wife as Princess of Soul". Mount Song has both the Shaolin Temple, a Buddhist holy place, and the Daoist Zhongyue Temple, and offering sacrifices on Mount Song can meet the demands of them both. Moreover, the choice of Mount Song also avoided the conflicts between Li Tang and Wu Zhou. After all, according to the interpretation of *Five Great Books of Righteousness*, the practice of worship on the mountain is a symbol of dynastic change and world peace. In 666 AD when Li Zhi offered sacrifices on Mount Tai, he was representing the Tang Dynasty of Li's family; so if Wu Zetian were to worship on Mount Tai, she would be representing Wuzhou, which meant that Wu Zetian had usurped the power of Li Zhi, and the conflict between Wu and Li would be brought to the surface. Being husband and wife, they were on the throne together when Li Zhi was in power as Emperor Gao, and worshiping again on Mount Tai meant that Wu Zetian was denying Li Zhi, which was also denying herself. In the feudal era when the authority of the husband prevailed in the culture, Wu Zetian could neither openly break with the Tang Dynasty nor engage Li Zhi as an opposing force. She could only keep herself away from this tough situation. Choosing Mount Song as the place of worship cleverly avoided the conflict between Li Tang and Wu Zhou as well as that between Li Zhi and Wu Zetian, and shunning this danger was conducive to the ensuing rule of Empress Wu.

五、洛阳牡丹甲天下

洛阳牡丹是中国的名花之一,它花朵硕大,花容端丽,雍容华贵,超逸群卉,素有"花王"之称。唐代以来,牡丹之盛,唯有洛阳,之后更以"洛阳牡丹甲天下"的美名流传于世。那么"洛阳牡丹甲天下"这句名言是什么时候开始流传的呢?

洛阳牡丹
Peony in Luoyang

牡丹原为野生的落叶小灌木,在中国大约有1500年的栽培历史。

V. The Peony in Luoyang is Second to None

The peony in Luoyang is one of China's famous flowers. It enjoys the fame of "Flora Queen" as its gorgeous petals strike an impressive scene and overshadow all other blooms. Since the Tang Dynasty, the city of Luoyang is the prime spot for this flower. The saying "The peony in Luoyang is second to none" is widespread all across the world. So when did this famous saying become popular?

As a wild deciduous shrub, the peony has been cultivated in China for about 1500 years. In the Han Dynasty, Liu Xiu once hid among peony blooms in Mituo Temple to avoid his rival Wang Mang's soldiers. After Liu Xiu became the emperor, he named the flower "Han Peony". During the Wei, Jin, and Southern and Northern dynasties, the peony began to be nurtured as an ornamental plant. In the Sui Dynasty, the number and variety of peony cultivation soared in a wide range. After Emperor Yang Guang succeeded to the throne in the Sui Dynasty, he opened a West Garden in Luoyang, the capital, to plant peonies. He collected peony varieties from all over the world to cultivate them. Every April, the capital was full of peonies. During the Tang Dynasty, peony planting continued to flourish, and there were also gardeners who specialized in planting peonies. Peonies could be seen everywhere in the palaces, temples and mansions.

The reputation of the statement "The peony in Luoyang is second to none" closely relates to Wu Zetian, the only empress in Chinese history. Wu Shu, a famous litterateur in the Northern Song Dynasty, noted in *Records of Eccentrics in the Yangtze and Huaihe Rivers*: "Empress Wu announced that she would visit Royal Gardens. All flowers were in full bloom while only peonies didn't blossom, so she punished peonies to be demoted to Luoyang. Later, Luoyang had the best peonies in the world." This actually presents a beautiful legend about peonies. In the season of snowstorm, Empress Wu Zetian suddenly ordered, "Tomorrow morning, I will visit Royal Gardens. Send an imperial edict to spring god to let him know. All flowers must bloom overnight. Don't wait until the morning wind blows." Once the imperial edict was issued, all flowers dared not disobey it. Only the peony insisted on blooming in the spring. Empress Wu was so furious that she ordered the peony to be demoted to Luoyang. Later, peonies took root in

汉代时，刘秀曾躲在弥陀寺的牡丹花间躲避王莽的追兵，称帝后，将该花赐名为"汉牡丹"。魏晋南北朝时期，牡丹开始作为观赏植物培养。隋代时，牡丹的栽培数量和种类大范围增加。隋炀帝杨广继位后，在东都洛阳开辟西苑专门种植牡丹，收集天下各色的牡丹品种来培植，每年四月的东都遍地开满牡丹。唐代时期，牡丹种植继续发展，还出现了专门种植牡丹的花匠，宫廷、寺院、府宅到处可见牡丹的踪迹。

"洛阳牡丹甲天下"的美誉，与中国历史上唯一的女皇帝武则天有着密切的联系。北宋著名文学家吴淑在《江淮异人录》中记载"武后诏游上苑，百花俱放，牡丹独迟，遂令贬于洛阳，后洛阳牡丹甲天下也"，这实际上记载了一个有关牡丹的美丽传说。大雪纷飞的季节，女皇武则天突然下令"明朝游上苑，火急报春知。花须连夜发，莫待晓风吹"。诏令一发，百花莫敢不从，唯有牡丹坚持在春日开放，武则天见牡丹不遵从自己的旨意勃然大怒，一声令下将牡丹贬到洛阳，后来牡丹在洛阳生根发芽，最终使得洛阳成为"牡丹花城"。这个典故从侧面体现出来武则天是洛阳牡丹的推动者，对唐及以后牡丹的发展都做出了卓越的贡献。

宋代以后洛阳被认为是种植牡丹的最佳地区。北宋的大文学家欧阳修曾说："洛阳地脉花最宜，牡丹尤为天下奇。"欧阳修还撰写了我国现存最早的一部关于牡丹的专著《洛阳牡丹记》，他对"洛阳牡丹甲天下"一说，做出了最全面最客观的阐释，详细地介绍了洛阳牡丹，肯定了洛阳牡丹天下第一的历史地位。除此之外，在这部最早的牡丹专著中，欧阳修明确表示，虽然其他地方也有牡丹，但只有洛阳的牡丹才能称为天下第一，并且还说只有牡丹才能算得上是真花，后人也多引用欧阳修这句"天下真花独牡丹"来称赞洛阳牡丹开花时的风姿绰约。

除欧阳修之外，还有许多历史人物对天下第一的洛阳牡丹进行赞美。南宋诗人陆游曾在《天彭牡丹谱》中写道"牡丹在中州，洛阳为第一"。明代，李贤、彭时等修撰《大明统一志》中记载："牡丹，出洛阳者为

Luoyang and eventually rendered Luoyang a "Peony City". This allusion shows that Empress Wu promoted Luoyang peony and made a difference to the growth of peony in the Tang Dynasty and later.

After the Song Dynasty, Luoyang was considered the best venue to plant peonies. Ouyang Xiu, a great writer of the Northern Song Dynasty, once said, "Luoyang is the most suitable place for local flowers, especially peonies." He also wrote the earliest existing monograph on the peony flower in China entitled *Story of Luoyang Peony*. He interpreted most comprehensively and objectively the saying that "The peony in Luoyang is second to none", introduced Luoyang peony in detail, and affirmed its historical status as the preeminent flower globally. In addition, in the earliest peony monograph, Ouyang Xiu made it clear that in spite of peonies in other places, only peonies in Luoyang can be called the best in the world. He also said that only peonies could be regarded as the Flora Queen. Later generations also cited Ouyang Xiu's saying that "Only peonies can enjoy the fame of Flora Queen" to praise the stunning view of Luoyang peonies when they bloom.

Besides Ouyang Xiu, numerous historical celebrities commended the Luoyang peony as the best in the world. Lu You, a poet of the Southern Song Dynasty, once wrote in *Tianpeng Peony Manual* that "Peonies in Luoyang in the Central Plains are the best". In the Ming Dynasty, Li Xian, Peng Shi and others recorded in the *Unified Annals of the Ming Dynasty* that "Peonies that come out of Luoyang are the best in the world". In the Qing Dynasty, the techniques of using peony fragrance to enrich tea aroma and ripening peony matured, and some methods have been applied to this day. After the People's Republic of China was founded, Premier Zhou Enlai once said during his visit to Luoyang, "The peony is the national flower of China. It is elegant, gorgeous and a symbol of prosperity and sweet happiness of our Chinese nation." Since then, the fame of Luoyang peony has spread all over the country.

The Luoyang peony has gone through countless dynasties, but its inheritance has never been interrupted. The inheritance of the Luoyang peony has not ceased in terms of its place in historical culture, varieties of cultivation, ornamental beautification, edible and medical value, use in scientific research and beneficial ecological function. Luoyang established the first Peony Research Institute, the

天下第一"。清代时期的牡丹熏花和催熟技术十分成熟，一些方法沿用至今。新中国成立后，周总理视察洛阳时曾说道："牡丹是我国的国花，它雍容华贵，富丽堂皇，是我们中华民族兴旺发达、美好幸福的象征。"自此，洛阳牡丹甲天下的名声传遍了全国。

洛阳牡丹历经多朝但从未中断传承，洛阳牡丹的历史文化、品种培育、观赏美化、食用药用、科研开发和生态建设等方面的传承也没有停歇。洛阳建立了国内第一个牡丹研究院、第一个国家牡丹基因库、第一个牡丹学院，在市区建设的各具特色的大型牡丹观赏园达15个，这些牡丹花园已经成为国内春季旅游的首选目的地。如今牡丹特色产业已经成为洛阳五大特色产业之一，牡丹产业链正在快速形成。中国洛阳牡丹文化节是洛阳每年最为盛大的节日，这是洛阳人的独特节日，更是全国观赏牡丹的盛宴。刘禹锡曾对牡丹进行了非常贴切的评价："庭前芍药妖无格，池上芙蕖净少情。唯有牡丹真国色，花开时节动京城。"洛阳牡丹值得"国色天香"的称赞。

隋唐时期是中国封建社会最为繁荣与开放的时期，中原文明则是这一时期最为耀眼的明珠。"营造东都""封禅嵩山""洛阳牡丹甲天下"是隋唐时期国家强盛、经济繁荣的象征，正是因为国家的统一、强大，才有了如此这番繁华的景象。"僧救唐王"则反映了隋唐交替之际，中原地区仍是各方争夺的战略之地。"玄奘取经"则是隋唐时期对外交往频繁的体现，后来衍生出的唐僧取经成为中国家喻户晓的神话故事。只有隋唐时期灿烂包容的文化和时代背景，才可以孕育出如此欣欣向荣的盛世局面。

first national peony gene bank, and the first peony college in China. There are 15 large peony gardens with unique features in Luoyang's urban area. These peony gardens have stood out as popular scenic spots for tourists in the spring. Today, the peony industry has become one of the five featured industries in Luoyang, and a relevant industrial chain is taking shape robustly. Each year witnesses the grandest festival called the Peony Culture Festival in Luoyang. It is a unique carnival for the locals and a feast for viewing peonies nationwide. Poet Liu Yuxi of the Tang Dynasty once commended peony highly: "Chinese herbaceous peonies in front of the court are enchanting, gorgeous but lack dignity. Lotuses in the pool are elegant, pure but lack charm. Only peonies, the matchless beauty, impress the whole capital in blossoming season." Luoyang's peony is worthy of the praise.

The Sui and Tang dynasties were the most prosperous and open period of Chinese feudal society, and the civilization of the Central Plains was the most dazzling pearl of this period. "Building the Eastern Capital", "Feng and Shan: Offering Sacrifices on Mount Song", and "The Peony in Luoyang is Second to None" are all expressions that symbolize China's prosperity and wealth in the Sui and Tang dynasties. Only a unified and powerful country can portray such a prosperous scene. "Shaolin Monks Rescuing the King of Tang" reflects that the Central Plains still acted as a strategic place for all parties at the turn of Sui and Tang Dynasties. The story of "Xuanzang Going to the West for the Buddhist Sutras" embodies the frequent foreign exchanges in the Sui and Tang dynasties. Later, the mythological version of Xuanzang's pilgrimage based on the actual story became a household tale in China. Only the brilliant and inclusive culture of the Sui and Tang dynasties could breed such a prosperous heyday.

第四章

宋元明清典故

Chapter 4

Allusions in Song, Yuan, Ming and Qing

Dynasties

宋元明清时期,包括宋朝、元朝、明朝、清朝四个朝代,从公元960年宋朝建立算起,至公元1911年清朝灭亡为止,共经历近一千年的历史。宋朝(公元960年—公元1279年)是中国历史上的黄金时期,分为北宋和南宋时期。北宋定都东京开封府(今河南开封),这一时期河南仍是整个中国的政治、文化中心。公元1127年,北宋灭亡后,南宋定都临安(今浙江杭州),元、明、清三代均定都北京,政治、经济重心逐渐从中原地区转移出去。

一、杯酒释兵权

有一句谚语讲道:篱笆筑得牢,邻居处得好。也就是说,只有完全消除产生矛盾的可能,人与人之间才能真正建立起最为和谐的关系。这种理念在权力的斗争中表现得更加强烈,中国古代的君主们就在这方面留下了许多故事,而杯酒释兵权就是其中非常具有代表性的例子。

宋朝是建立在唐朝之后的一个新兴的统一王朝。唐朝后期中央政府力量孱弱,因此各地藩镇将领相互征伐,都希望能入主中原,统一天下。

杯酒释兵权
Releasing the Military Power by Winning and Dining

Song, Yuan, Ming and Qing dynasties cover a history over one millennium from 960 AD when the Song Dynasty was established to 1911 AD when the Qing Dynasty came to an end. The Song Dynasty (960 AD-1279 AD) was a golden era in Chinese history that split into the Northern and Southern Song dynasties. In the first half of the Song, China pivoted on Henan Province politically and culturally during the Northern Song Dynasty with Kaifeng City as its capital (now Kaifeng, Henan Province). The year 1127 AD witnessed the demise of the Northern Song Dynasty while the Southern Song Dynasty shifted its capital to Lin'an City (now Hangzhou, Zhejiang Province). Later Beijing rose to be the new capital in Yuan, Ming and Qing dynasties. Thus political and economic focus drifted away from the Central Plains bit by bit.

I. Releasing the Military Power by Wining and Dining

A proverb says: "Good fences make good neighbors." In other words, people can enjoy the soundest relationship only by completely eliminating sparks of conflicts. This idea manifests itself most clearly in the struggle for power. Ancient Chinese monarchs left a variety of stories in this regard, and the story of releasing the military power by wining and dining is a typical example which took place in the Song Dynasty.

The Song Dynasty became a new unified period after the Tang Dynasty. In the late Tang Dynasty, the central government was feeble, so generals of various towns and cities fought against each other, hoping to take control of the Central Plains and unify the nation. Before the Song Dynasty, the Central Plains suffered a long period of war and turmoil. During this period, some regimes unified the country for short periods, and then they vanished in coups and wars, such as the Later Liang Dynasty, Later Tang Dynasty, Later Jin Dynasty, Later Han Dynasty and Later Zhou Dynasty. However, General Zhao Kuangyin's presence ended all this chaos. Zhao was originally a general of the Later Zhou Dynasty. In 959 AD, Emperor Chai Rong died of illness so the throne was passed to his youngest son, a child of only seven years old. The power was in the hands of the lad's grandma, Ms. Fu. But Grandma Fu didn't possess adequate political wisdom to rule the nation. Just then the rumor that the Northern Liao Kingdom would

到宋朝建立之前，中原大地上经历了长时期的战争与动乱，这一时期虽然陆续出现了一些实现短暂统一的政权，主要有后梁、后唐、后晋、后汉、后周等，但是很快它们都在政变与战争中毁灭，一直到赵匡胤出现才结束了这场乱局。赵匡胤本来是后周的大将，公元959年，世宗柴荣积劳成疾病逝，皇位传给了只有七岁的小儿子，而由符太后主政，符太后政治能力不高，致使政局不稳。恰好此时又传来北方辽国入侵的谣言，朝中大臣皆鼓吹应对乱局者唯有赵匡胤一人，无奈之下符太后只能授予赵匡胤调动全国军队的权力。赵匡胤在掌握了兵权以后，率大军出征，随后军队行至陈桥驿（今河南封丘陈桥镇）时，他的手下石守信、赵普等人便煽动士兵发动兵变，拥戴赵匡胤为皇帝，赵匡胤假意推辞一番后便坦然接受了。兵变成功后，赵匡胤立即率领部队返回了东京开封府（今河南开封），在他的逼迫下，年幼的皇帝只好将皇位传给了他。

　　赵匡胤是依靠军事政变获得皇位的，因此他一直非常担心别人也用同样的方法来夺取自己的皇位。他询问自己非常信任的大臣赵普说："从唐朝的后期到现在，天下出现了无休无止的战争，我从乱世中走出来，只希望我的王朝能够长治久安，天下再无动乱发生，这如何实现还请先生教我。"赵普本身就一直在谋划这个事情，因此他赶忙回答道："陛下，动乱发生得如此频繁，都是因为藩镇将军们的力量太过强大，如果想要国家长治久安，就要削弱地方藩镇行政、征税的权力，使他们掌握少量的士兵，这样地方就无法发动叛乱与政变了。"赵普提出的方法深得赵匡胤的认同，但是那些掌握权力的将领们都是跟随赵匡胤很久的部下，他们平时没有大的过错，对赵匡胤也没有任何不忠的举动，因此赵匡胤还是不相信他们会背叛自己，他对赵普说："众将军跟随我多年，必不会叛我，先生不必怀疑。"但是赵普回答道："陛下，将军们不会有反叛之心，但是倘若他们掌控不好自己的军队，使得某些心怀叵测之人借机行事，强迫他们叛乱，那时他们亦是无能为力。"赵普的话引起了赵匡胤的警惕，他下定了决心准备收回兵权。

invade became known. Ministers in the palace all insisted that only General Zhao Kuangyin could rise to the occasion and settle the chaos. Hence Grandma Fu had no choice but to grant General Zhao the power to mobilize the national army. When General Zhao took control of the military power, he led a large troop to fight. When the troops went to Chenqiaoyi (now Chenqiao Town, Fengqiu, Henan Province), his subordinates including Shi Shouxin and Zhao Pu incited soldiers to launch a mutiny and supported General Zhao to be the emperor. After pretending to refuse, General Zhao accepted this appointment gladly. Upon the victorious mutiny, General Zhao led his troops back to the capital at Kaifeng (now Kaifeng, Henan Province). Under his coercion, the young emperor had to relinquish the throne to him.

Since Emperor Zhao ascended to the throne by a military coup, he always worried that others would use the same method to seize his throne. He asked Minister Zhao Pu whom he trusted deeply: "The nation suffered endless strife from the late Tang Dynasty till now. I have come out of troubled times, so I just hope that my dynasty can enjoy perennial stability and there will be no more unrest in the world. Please teach me how to achieve this." Minister Zhao himself had been planning for this possibility, so he hurriedly replied: "Your Majesty, frequent occurrence of unrest is due to the strength of local generals. Perennial stability of the country comes from weakening administrative and taxation power of local generals. They cannot launch a rebellion or coup with only a limited number of soldiers." This method won the emperor's approval. However, generals who had been in power for a long time composed his subordinates. They committed no major mistakes and had no disloyalty to him. Therefore, he still did not believe that they would betray him. He said to Zhao Pu: "Those generals have supported me for many years, and they will not betray me. Minister, about this there is no doubt." But Zhao Pu replied: "Your Majesty, the generals will not have the desire to rebel, but if they can't control their own troops well and someone with ulterior motives seizes the chance to force them to rebel, they might seize the opportunity at that time." Those words aroused Emperor Zhao's vigilance. He made up his mind to take back the military power.

At last, the chance presented itself for the emperor at a wine party. While drunk, the emperor suddenly complained to his generals: "I could not have

终于在一次酒会上赵匡胤找到了机会，酒酣之时，赵匡胤忽然抱怨道："我能有今日之成就，离不开诸位的效命，为此我心怀感激，但是如今我虽为皇帝，却深感焦虑，每夜都睡不安稳，倒不如当初当将军时快乐。"众将领听到皇帝苦恼连忙询问说："不知道陛下因何事愁闷呢？"赵匡胤趁机说道："人人都知道皇帝独断乾坤，这样的地位，谁不想拥有呢？"众将军一听此话非常惶恐，连忙跪地向皇帝表达忠心，说道："陛下此话怎讲，如今天下已经安定，何人敢反抗圣上？"赵匡胤说道："我亦深知诸位的忠心，但是假如有一天你们的手下生出谋逆之心，逼迫你们起兵，诸位即便不愿意，又当如何制止呢？"众将军更害怕了，连忙询问赵匡胤："我等不知陛下竟有这样的担忧，恳请陛下示下，如何才能解除这后顾之忧。"赵匡胤随后对他们说道："人的一生如白驹过隙，匆匆而逝，每个人所追求的，不过就是多多积攒财富，为子孙后代谋一个好前程，你们不如放弃手里的军权，多购买土地房屋，为自己的后代留下产业，自己也多买些歌女舞姬，安度晚年。我与诸位结为儿女亲家，这样大家没有了猜疑，岂不是再无后顾之忧？"众将军此时都明白了皇帝的意思，于是都寻找理由上书向皇帝请辞，而赵匡胤也欣然同意，同时趁机进行了制度改革，大力削弱高级军事职务的权力，维持了王朝长期的稳定。

赵匡胤的方法虽然在一定程度上纵容了部下贪污腐败，但是他巧妙地使用了谋略，在没有引发争斗的前提下，用和平手段解除了部下的权力威胁，成功地防止了未来可能发生的兵变，彻底结束了从唐朝后期频繁发生的叛乱行为。

杯酒释兵权的故事展现了中国古人对于权力的认识，以及对于权力斗争产生原因的分析与应对。中国古人相信权力的归属不明会引起频繁的动乱，同时矛盾发生的根源在于利益的冲突，而政治斗争的出现很多时候也是因为权力受到了威胁。在面对危急时，分析危急产生的根源，寻找最为温和的手段，将危急的解决限制在可控的范围内，这是中国古人应对问题的智慧。

achieved what I am today without your service. For this reason, I am grateful. But now, as the emperor, I am deeply concerned. I can't sleep well every night. I'm not so happy as when I was a general." Hearing this, the generals quickly inquired, "Why is Your Majesty depressed?" The emperor took the opportunity to say, "Everyone knows that the emperor has the final say. Who doesn't crave such a position?" The remark frightened the generals who knelt down to express loyalty and said, "Your Majesty, now the nation is stable, who dares to revolt against you?" The emperor replied, "I also know your loyalty, but if one day your subordinates turned rebellious and forced you to revolt, how could you stop them even if you didn't want to rebel yourself?" The generals were even more scared and said, "We have no idea Your Majesty has such worries. Please let us know how to relieve these worries." The emperor then replied: "A person's life passes like a fleeting moment in time. What everyone pursues is to win more wealth and seek a promising prospect for future generations. You might as well give up your military power, buy more real-estate and houses, leave lands for the following generations, and purchase singers and dancers to spend your old age in peace. I will arrange my kids to marry yours, so you will be free from doubts and worries." Now the emperor made himself clear, so generals all resigned by writing under the guise of excuses, to which the emperor readily agreed. Meanwhile, Emperor Zhao launched systemic reform, weakened authority of senior military posts, and maintained perennial stability of the dynasty.

Although his method condoned corruption of his subordinates to a certain extent, Zhao used a smart strategy to get rid of the threat of his generals' mutiny and did so by peaceful means without provoking strife. He prevented possible coups in the future, and ended frequent rebellions in the late Tang Dynasty once for all.

The story of releasing the military power by wining and dining shows the ancient Chinese recognition of power, as well as skillful analysis and response to the reasons for power struggle. Ancient Chinese believed that unclear ownership of power would give rise to frequent unrest. Meanwhile, the root of contradictions was conflicting interests, and political struggle occurred often because power was threatened. In the face of a crisis, it is the wisdom of ancient Chinese to analyze its root causes and find the most moderate means to limit crisis to a controllable range.

二、程门立雪

尊师重道是中华民族的优良传统美德，即每个学生要在言行举止上尊重老师，要在求学问道中尊重知识。中国历史历久弥新，洗练出无数尊师重道的经典故事。在宋代，嵩阳书院就曾发生过这样一件尊师重道的故事，人们称它为"程门立雪"。

程门立雪
Standing in the Snow to Wait upon Master Cheng

嵩阳书院位于嵩山，在中国古人的历史地理观中，嵩山便是天地的中心，被称为"天地之中"。在这得天独厚的环境中，嵩阳书院传承着天地灵气。特别是"二程"（程颢和程颐）的到来，为这片土地赋予了更多的人文内涵，吸引了更多的文人学者前来求学，杨时和游酢也在其中，他们两人就是"程门立雪"这个故事的主人翁。

II. Standing in the Snow to Wait upon Master Cheng

Respecting teachers proves to be a traditional virtue of the Chinese. Every student shall respect teachers in words and deeds, and respect knowledge in learning. China's history is everlastingly new. It has nurtured countless classic stories of respecting teachers. Such a story is associated with the Songyang Academy in the Song Dynasty and is called "Standing in the Snow to Wait upon Master Cheng".

Songyang Academy is situated on Mount Song. In the historical and geographical view of ancient Chinese, Mount Song was the center of the heaven and the earth, known as the "Center of the Universe". Hence Songyang Academy inherited the spirit of the heaven and the earth in this unique surrounding. In particular, the arrival of two masters—Cheng Hao and Cheng Yi endowed this academy with humanistic connotations and attracted great numbers of learners to study. Yang Shi and You Zuo, protagonists of the story, were among them.

Yang Shi was smart from an early age. He could write poetry at the age of seven and prose at eight. He was called a "prodigy" by villagers. When he grew up, he won the title of Jinshi (a successful candidate in the highest imperial examinations). Yet, to pursue more profound knowledge, he acknowledged Cheng Hao as his teacher by studying hard and becoming knowledgeable. However, when Cheng Hao died, Yang refused to give up his pursuit of wisdom. His good friend You Zuo was impressed by his perseverance and often discussed academic issues with him. One day, they encountered a thorny problem in their discussions. You Zuo proposed to consult Master Cheng Yi. Just then, Yang Shi also expressed his wish to venerate Cheng Yi as his teacher. The two hit it off and set out to find Master Cheng. However, the journey of their pursuit of wisdom was not so easy as expected.

It was a cold winter. Braving the bitter cold, they arrived at Songyang Academy early in the morning. Unfortunately, Cheng Yi was meditating with his eyes closed. The two arrivals thought that they would wait for a while, and then enter the room to ask questions after the teacher finished his meditation. However, the weather got worse. Bigger and denser snowflakes were falling from

杨时小时候聪明伶俐，七岁能写诗，八岁就会作赋，被乡亲们称为"神童"。他长大后，又考中了进士。但是为了追求更高深的学问，他拜大学者程颢为师，刻苦钻研学问，收获了不少知识。但是，后来程颢去世了，他又不肯放弃对知识的追逐。而游酢作为杨时的好朋友，看到杨时这样坚持，被他的求学精神打动，经常与他一起探讨学术。有一天，杨时和游酢在讨论的过程中遇到一个比较棘手的问题，游酢便提议去请教一下程颐先生。恰好，杨时此时也正有拜程颐为师的想法。两人一拍即合，便出发去寻找程颐。但是，他们二人的拜师之旅并没有想象中那么容易。

那是一个寒冷的冬天，杨时和游酢冒着严寒，一大早就来到了嵩阳书院。不巧的是，程颐当时正在闭着眼睛打坐。杨时和游酢就想着稍等一会儿，等老师静坐完毕之后再入室请教问题。可是天公不作美，天上飘起了雪花，并且越下越大，越下越密，不一会儿，地上、房上和树上都堆上了厚厚一层雪，气温也一下子降低了很多。但他们怕打扰老师静修，既不愿意进入较为暖和的书房等候，也不愿意轻易放弃这次求学的机会，就在客厅恭敬地等候。就这样，时间一点点地过去。等到程颐从书房出来发现杨时和游酢这两个人的时候，门外积雪已有一尺多深，但他们二人却仍然静立如初，面色也没有透露出一点不耐烦，反而更加恭敬地向老师作揖请教。这让程颐很感动，于是程颐便将他们视为自己的得意门生，悉心教导。在此之后，杨、游二人果然不负所望，刻苦学习，终于成为一代理学大师。

在这个故事中，老师做到了言传身教，学生也能够尊师重道，是教育史上难能可贵的教学案例。从古至今，被传为佳话的名人尊师范例也不胜枚举。新中国成立后，毛主席回到阔别三十二年的故乡韶山，他特意邀请自己在私塾读书时的毛禹珠老师一起用饭，席间还热情地为老师敬酒，毛禹珠感慨地说："主席敬酒，岂敢岂敢！"毛主席却笑盈盈地回答："敬老尊贤，应该应该。"鲁迅先生也常在百忙中抽空探望老师。鲁迅对私塾老师寿镜吾先生一直很尊敬，他十八岁到南京读书，每当放

the sky. After a while, a thick layer of snow shrouded the ground, the houses and the trees. It became unbearably freezing. Afraid to disturb the teacher's meditation, they didn't enter the warmer study area to wait, nor did they give up the chance to study, so they waited respectfully in the living room. Time passed by. When Master Cheng came out of his study and saw them, the snow outside mounted to more than a foot deep. However, they were standing still without any impatience on their faces. Instead, they bowed respectfully to the Master for advice. This impressed Cheng Yi, so he regarded them as his favorite students and taught them with his heart and soul. After that, the two learners lived up to expectations, studied hard, and eventually became Masters of Neo-Confucianism.

In this story, the teacher taught by example and students respected their teachers, which is a valuable model in the history of education. Numerous examples of celebrities honoring teachers are well known throughout the Chinese history. After the founding of People's Republic of China, Chairman Mao returned to his hometown Shaoshan from which he had been away for 32 years. There he treated Mao Yuzhu—his teacher in the old-style private school, to dinner. During dinner, he made a warm toast to his teacher. Mao Yuzhu sighed, "I'm so flattered by a toast from the Chairman!" Chairman Mao smiled and said: "I respect and honor the aged and the wise as you are." Mr. Lu Xun, a writer, often visited his teachers in spite of a busy schedule. He respected his private school teacher, Mr. Shou Jingwu. Lu Xin went to study in Nanjing at the age of 18. The writer managed to visit Mr. Shou whenever he returned to his hometown Shaoxing on the holidays, no matter how busy he was. Later, He studied in Japan for eight years. Lu Xun often wrote letters to Mr. Shou to report his study. He was a typical example of "respecting one's teacher during one's lifetime".

The reason why we emphasize respect for teachers is that respect for teachers, education, wisdom and learning is one of the finest traditions of the Chinese. Since Confucius founded the first school in Qufu, Shandong Province, respecting teachers has been practiced for thousands of years. The status of teachers is equal to that of the "heaven, earth, sovereign and parent". Even emperors should worship Confucius when they meet "the exemplary teacher for all ages". This thought has been passed down in traditional feudal society. In the Tang Dynasty, Emperor Taizong highlighted education for his own children and taught them

假回绍兴，不论多忙，总要抽空去看望寿老先生。后来，鲁迅远涉重洋，东渡日本留学，这八年间，鲁迅还经常写信向寿老师汇报自己在异土的学习情况，真正做到了"一入师门，终生不忘"。

我们之所以如此强调尊师重道，是因为尊师重教、崇智尚学是中华民族的优良传统。自孔子在山东曲阜开创第一所学校以来，尊师之风传承千年。这时候老师的地位是和"天、地、君、亲"平齐的，就连皇帝见到孔子这种"万世师表"也要顶礼膜拜。这种思想一直在传统封建社会传承。在唐朝的时候，唐太宗非常重视对子女的教育，而且教导他们一定要尊重老师。有一次，他们的老师李纲患了脚疾，不方便走路。唐太宗就特许李纲可以坐轿进入皇宫内，并命令皇子们出门迎接。但是这种情况到了元代开始改变，老师的地位明显下降。据史籍记载，由于元代是由北方少数民族蒙古族建立的统一的王朝国家，面对经济文化相对发达的汉族地区，实行了一系列打压汉人的政策，把以教书为生的儒士降为社会阶层中的下等人，教师的地位明显下降。之后，清代再次确定了"天地君亲师"的次序，特别突出了"师"的地位和作用。慢慢地发展到民国时期，教师地位有所提高。特别是新中国成立以后，1951年，中华人民共和国教育部、中华全国总工会共同商定，将"教师节"与"五一国际劳动节"合并在一起，教师地位重新得到确立。随后在中国便掀起了一阵有关"教师节"的热烈讨论，社会上先后出现以"马克思的诞辰5月5日""孔子的诞辰9月28日"定为"教师节"等的提法，直到1985年才逐渐确定每年的9月10日为"教师节"。社会对于"教师节"日期的讨论从侧面也正好说明了尊师重道的传统在当下的社会正在逐渐恢复生机。

然而，对于尊师重道的提倡并不等同于盲目推行跪拜礼等繁文缛节。在今天，发扬尊师重教的传统既有利于建设社会美德，更有助于推动教育事业的发展、提高人口素质，从而为祖国建设培养更多、更优秀的人才。所以，尊师重道的优良传统永远不能丢、永远不能忘。只有教育才是承载民族的希望和未来，强国必先重教，重教必须尊师。

to respect their teachers. Once, their teacher Li Gang suffered from foot disease, and was unable to walk. The Emperor authorized Li Gang to enter the palace by sedan chair and ordered the princes to go out to welcome him. But the status of teachers declined sharply after the Yuan Dynasty. According to historical files, the Mongolian minority in the north established the Yuan Dynasty, and they suppressed the Han people by a series of policies because the latter enjoyed relatively developed economy and culture. Moreover, Mongolians belittled scholars who taught for a living as lower class in the society. Hence the status of teachers dropped sharply. Later, it was not until the Qing Dynasty that the order of the "heaven, earth, sovereign, parent and teacher" was resumed again. Highlighting the status and role of teachers improved in slow progression down to the Republic of China, when the status of teachers improved. The turning point appeared after the founding of People's Republic of China. In 1951, the new nation's Ministry of Education and All-China Federation of Trade Unions settled to combine "Teachers' Day" with "International Workers' Day (May 1)", thus the status of teachers was reaffirmed. Subsequently, a heated discussion about the date of "Teachers' Day" occurred in China. A variety of proposals showed up, such as "Marx's birthday—May 5" and "Confucius' birthday—September 28". It was not until 1985 that September 10 of each year was gradually determined as Teachers' Day. Discussion on the date of Teachers' Day also presents that tradition of respecting teachers and valuing morality is gaining momentum in current society.

However, advocating respect for teachers doesn't equal blindly carrying out such red tape as kneeling. Promoting the tradition of respecting teachers and valuing education today is not only conducive to building social virtues, but also facilitates growth of education and quality among the population, so as to cultivate more and better talents for building the motherland. Therefore, the fine tradition of respecting teachers and morality should never be lost or forgotten. Only education carries hope and future of the nation. A strong country comes from quality education which grows from respecting teachers.

三、精忠报国

精忠报国
Serving the Country Faithfully

  图中展示的是一幅庙宇中的壁画，这座庙宇位于河南省安阳市汤阴县，名字叫作"岳飞庙"。几乎每一个中国人，即使是一个儿童，看到这幅画都会马上理解其含义，并可以向你解释其内容。图片上半跪着的青年是中国历史上最著名的将军之一岳飞，后面站着拿针的妇人是他的母亲，他背上的四个汉字即是：精忠报国。
  岳飞战斗在金人南侵的时代，他在抗金战争中取得的成绩、他属下军队严明的纪律以及他被昏君奸臣出卖的结局，使他成为一个充满悲剧化色彩的英雄。精忠报国的故事之所以流传如此广泛，是因为中国人民

Ⅲ. Serving the Country Faithfully

The picture shows a mural in a temple located in Tangyin County, Anyang City, Henan Province. The temple is called "Yuefei Temple". Almost every Chinese person, even a child, understands the meaning of this painting and can explain its essence to you. The young man half-kneeling in the picture is Yue Fei, one of the most renowned generals in Chinese history. The woman standing behind him with a needle is his mother. The Chinese characters on his back read as follows: " 精忠报国 " (Serve the Country Faithfully).

Yue Fei fought in the period of the Jin people's invasion of China. He became a tragic hero because of his achievements in the war against Jin, strict discipline of his troops, and his death at the hands of tyrants and treacherous ministers. The popularity of his story reflects that Chinese people hold him in high esteem, an expression of their patriotism to a large extent, which has been the case since ancient times.

A loud cry of a newborn came from a farmhouse of a Yue family in Tangyin County (today's Tangyin County, Anyang City) on the night of February 25, 1103 AD. This newborn was Yue Fei. At that time, there happened to be a big bird chirping on his house, so his family named him "Fei" (which means flying in Chinese). As an ordinary farmer, he started physical labor at a young age, which endowed him with a robust body. In his spare time, he studied in seasonal schools in the rural areas in winter, and learned from others the fighting skills of archery and spear. Yue Fei joined the army and fought in the war against the northern Liao Dynasty in 1122 AD (the fourth year of Xuanhe reign of Emperor Huizong of the Song Dynasty). The newly arisen Jin army invaded the Song Dynasty and besieged the capital Bianliang (now Kaifeng City, Henan Province) for the second time in 1126 AD (the first year of Jingkang reign of Emperor Qinzong of the Song Dynasty). At that time, Yue Fei, as a cavalry team leader, was fighting against the Jin army in Shanxi Province. After the Northern Song army failed, Yue Fei had to escape to his hometown with his family. On the way home, Yue Fei, his wife and children suffered a lot. The scenes they saw were nothing but broken landscapes and victims in pain, which was like a knife piercing their

对岳飞的推崇。而推崇这位英雄，很大程度上是在表达他们朴素的爱国主义感情，从古到今都是这样。

宋徽宗赵佶崇宁二年（公元1103年）二月十五日夜里，相州汤阴县（今安阳市汤阴县）的一所岳姓人家的农舍中传来新生儿响亮的哭声。这个婴儿即是岳飞——当时恰好有大鸟飞鸣于其屋上，故岳家为他取名为"飞"。作为一个普通的农家孩子，岳飞从小开始体力劳动自然是其本分，在劳动中，岳飞练出了强壮的身体。在农闲时间，他在业余冬学中读书，并向他人学习射箭、矛术等战斗技能。宋徽宗宣和四年（公元1122年），岳飞投军，参与了和北方辽朝的战争。宋钦宗靖康元年（公元1126年），新兴起的金朝军队南侵，第二次包围京师汴梁（今河南省开封市）。当时岳飞作为一名骑兵小队长正在山西与金军对抗，北宋军队全线失败后，岳飞不得不带着家人奔回故乡。在归途中，岳飞和妻儿受尽苦楚，极目所见都是山河破碎、人民涂炭的景象。他们历尽千辛万苦，终于挣扎回到了汤阴，而故乡的情况也并不比外地好多少。女真铁骑所过之处，老弱惨遭杀害，妇女被驱掠，男子多被掳去充当苦力。幸运的是，岳飞见到了怀念已久的老母姚氏，总算得到了一点宽慰。在山西的战役中，岳飞已成为了身经百战的勇士。战友和百姓们的牺牲使他更强烈地感到愤怒，他渴望重返前线，为光复河山而效命。

但他有一个顾虑，那就是年过六十的老母亲。岳飞离家后，他的母亲姚氏，自然缺少照顾和保护，这让岳飞深感愧疚。姚氏是个普通的农家妇女，但她深明大义，决不愿意拖累儿子，而是积极勉励岳飞"从戎报国"。最后，岳飞决定留下妻子刘氏，照顾老母。

岳飞临行之际，姚氏在岳飞背上深深地刺了四个大字——"精忠报国"（史实为尽忠报国）。这四个字不仅刻在岳飞的背上，也刻在了他的心中。在往后的战斗岁月里，岳飞始终以百折不挠的努力，履践着自己和母亲共同的庄严誓言。他此后一生与金军斗争，渐渐凭借军功由一名低级军官升为南宋最重要的将领。他麾下的岳家军享有盛名，被对手

hearts. They went through hardships and finally struggled to return to Tangyin, where the situation in their hometown was not much better. Wherever the Jin cavalry intruded, the old and the weak were killed, women were snatched, and most of men were enslaved as laborers. Fortunately, Yue Fei felt relieved to meet his long cherished mother, Ms. Yao. In the battle of Shanxi, Yue Fei became an experienced warrior. The sacrifice of his comrades and fellow Chinese made him more furious. He was eager to return to the front line and serve the nation faithfully.

But one headache blocked him. His mother was over 60 years old. Upon his departure, his mother, Ms. Yao, naturally lacked care and protection, which made Yue Fei feel guilty. Ms. Yao, as an ordinary peasant, knew the great cause to which her son was committed and was never willing to be a millstone around her son's neck. Instead, she encouraged the warrior to "serve the country in the army". Eventually, Yue Fei decided to leave his wife Liu to take care of his mother.

When Yue Fei was about to leave, Ms. Yao tattooed four big characters on his back—"精忠报国"("Serve the Country Faithfully". The historical fact is that "the four characters are" 尽忠报国 ", literally, "Serve the Country Wholeheartedly").

These four characters were not only engraved on his back, but also in his heart. Yue Fei always carried out the sacred oath shared by him and his mother with indomitable efforts in the following years of fighting. He rose from a junior officer to the most important general in the Southern Song Dynasty as he fought against the Jin army all his life. The Yue family army under his command enjoyed a reputation on both sides of the war, and the evaluation of them was that it was "easier to shake mountains than to defeat the Yue family army". Yue Fei proposed many times to Emperor Zhao Gou, the founding father of the Southern Song Dynasty, to oppose peace talks with the Jin Dynasty, but was always rejected by the Emperor and Prime Minister Qin Hui. Wanyan Wuzhu (later known by his Chinese name Zongbi) of the Jin Dynasty tore up a peace treaty and invaded the Song Dynasty in 1140 AD (the 10th year of Shaoxing reign of Emperor Gaozong of the Song Dynasty). Yue Fei sent generals to contact a volunteer army in the north and let them attack the rear of the Jin army according to the general plan of "connecting the north and marching into the Central Plains". He defeated the

评价为"撼山易，撼岳家军难"。他多次向南宋的开国皇帝——宋高宗赵构上书，反对与金朝议和，但均遭到了赵构和宰相秦桧的拒绝。宋高宗绍兴十年（公元1140年），金朝的完颜宗弼撕毁和约，领兵南侵。岳飞按照"联结北方，进军中原"的方略，派遣将领联络北方的义军，让他们袭扰金军的后方。自己则率领岳家军的主力北上，在民众配合下充分发挥自身的战斗力，先后在郾城战役、颍昌战役中击败金军主力部队。

正当金军士气溃散，岳飞准备渡河北上收复失地时，宋高宗和秦桧却向金朝乞和，连下十几道旨意命令岳飞班师，岳飞的北伐事业最终失败。绍兴十一年（公元1141年），岳飞回到南宋首都临安（今浙江省杭州市），被解除了兵权。当年十月，秦桧等人设置冤狱，诬陷囚禁了岳飞。开始由一个名叫何铸的官员审问岳飞，岳飞撕裂衣服露出背上"精忠报国"四个字让何铸观看，为自己辩护，在场的人无不动容，何铸也上报岳飞的无辜。但宋高宗和秦桧等人一心要置岳飞于死地，以便与金朝议和，最终还是改派审判官，以"莫须有"的罪名将岳飞杀害。宋高宗绍兴十一年（公元1141年），岳飞在临安大理寺狱被杀害，同时遇害的还有他的儿子岳云和部将张宪。

岳飞冤死之时，上到皇族高官、下到军人百姓的广泛群体为其鸣不平。宋孝宗即位后，终于为岳飞平反昭雪。此后，不仅南宋统治者多次加封岳飞，之后的元明清各代皇帝也对其进行加封纪念。除了在其出生地汤阴和遇害地杭州有岳飞庙外，还有很多岳飞庙遍布大江南北。这些岳飞庙中少不了岳母刺字"精忠报国"雕塑、壁画。

千百年来，"精忠报国"成了中华民族爱国主义的一面旗帜。"国"指的就是中国，文化意义上的中国。对国家忠诚，为国家奉献，无数中国人在"精忠报国"这面旗帜的鼓舞下前仆后继，为国家贡献出自己的青春与生命，他们就是中华民族的脊梁。

main force of the Jin army in the battles of Yicheng and Yancheng by heading the main force of the Yue family army northward, and giving full play to their fighting capacity with the cooperation of local fighters.

Just as the morale of the Jin army collapsed and Yue Fei was about to recover lost territory by crossing over the river to Hebei Province, the Emperor and Prime Minister Qin Hui begged for peace with the Jin Dynasty and ordered Yue Fei to retreat by issuing a dozen decrees. Hence Yue Fei's Northern Expedition failed. He returned to Lin'an, capital of the Southern Song Dynasty (now Hangzhou, Zhejiang Province), and was relieved of his military power in 1141 AD (the 11th year of Shaoxing reign). Qin Hui and others set up an unjust lawsuit and imprisoned Yue Fei in October of that year. At first, an official named He Zhu interrogated Yue Fei. Yue Fei tore his clothes and revealed the characters "精忠报国" on his back and defended himself. That impressed everyone present, and interrogator He Zhu also reported Yue Fei's innocence. However, the Emperor, Qin Hui and others were determined to kill Yue Fei in order to make peace with the Jin Dynasty. In the end, they sent another interrogator to kill Yue Fei on the basis of a "groundless" accusation. Yue Fei was executed in the Dali Temple Prison in Lin'an in 1142 AD (the 11th year of Shaoxing reign, Emperor Gaozong of the Song Dynasty). Meanwhile, his son Yue Yun and subordinate Zhang Xian were also killed.

When Yue Fei died unjustly, a wide range of people, from senior officials of the royal family to soldiers and civilians, complained about his grievances. After Emperor Xiaozong ascended the throne, he eventually rehabilitated Yue Fei. Since then, not only rulers of the Southern Song Dynasty but also Emperors of Yuan, Ming and Qing dynasties granted titles and honors to him. Yuefei temples sprung up nationwide, including in his hometown of Tangyin and in Hangzhou, where he was killed. A sculpture mural portraying his mother tattooing "精忠报国" on his back is an integral part of the temples.

Hence "Serving the Country Faithfully" has become a banner of patriotism of the Chinese for thousands of years. "Country" here refers to China, a civilization. Countless Chinese talents, inspired by the passion of "Serving the Country Faithfully", have contributed their youth and lives to the country, serving the country loyally. They are the backbone of the Chinese nation.

四、许衡不食无主之梨

儒学是中国古代社会的主流文化,在儒学史上有一位被称为"元朝一人"的大儒许衡。许衡是中国宋末元初杰出的政治家、教育家、思想家和天文学家,是一位能够身体力行的学术大师,对理学的传播做出了很大贡献。

许衡1209年出生于河南新郑,许衡家族世代务农,但他自幼勤读好学,天资聪颖,7岁入学时,就曾问老师为何要读书,老师回答道:"是为了考科举。"许衡又问:"难道仅仅是这样?"老师大为惊异。由此可见,许衡认为读书并不仅仅是为了科举和做官,还应该有更高的追求。

许衡不食无主之梨

Xu Heng Wouldn't Eat Pears without the Owner's Permission

IV. Xu Heng Wouldn't Eat Pears Without the Owner's Permission

Confucianism is the mainstream culture of ancient Chinese society. A great Confucian Xu Heng enjoyed the reputation of being "The First Scholar in the Yuan Dynasty" in the history of Confucianism. Xu Heng, an outstanding politician, educator, thinker and astronomer in the end of the Song Dynasty and the early Yuan Dynasty, was an academic master who could practice earnestly what he advocated and made an important contribution to the popularity of Neo-Confucianism.

Xu Heng was born in Xinzheng, Henan Province in 1209 AD. His family had been farmers for generations, but he was studious and intelligent since his childhood. When he was seven years old, he asked the teacher why he should study. The latter replied, "For the imperial exams." Xu Heng asked again, "Is it only for this?" This impressed the teacher. It can be seen that Xu Heng believed that studying was not only for taking the imperial exams and being an official, but also for higher pursuits. As he progressed, Xu Heng would figure out every puzzle whenever he attended lectures, so his teacher said to his parents, "Your smart son is beyond my teaching competence. Please find him more competent teachers." Then the teacher bade everyone goodbye and left. Thus Xu Heng changed three teachers in a row. He became more studious as he grew up. He often traveled an arduous journey to borrow and copy books because his poor family couldn't afford them. He once saw a book explaining *The Book of Documents* in a fortune teller's home, then went back to copy it and read it attentively. Later, when he fled to Shandong Province, he got a *Book of Changes* annotated by the philosopher Wang Bi, which he read with all his heart and soul. Even in hard times, Xu Heng still insisted on reading day and night and practicing what he had learned, although the nation itself was in chaos.

At the end of the Southern Song Dynasty, Xu Heng fled with his fellows. They crossed a river in Luoyang and passed by a town named Heyang. It was a hot summer, and the scorching sun roasted the earth like a fireball. They were sweating and thirsty because of their exhausting journeys. At this time, a man saw a pear

以后每次老师讲书，许衡都要问个究竟，以至于老师对其父母说"令郎聪敏过人，我不能胜任，请别求名师"，便辞别而去，像这样连换了三位老师。许衡长大后更加好学，因家贫无钱购书，常跋涉百里借书抄书。他曾在一个算命先生家中看到一部解释《尚书》的书，便去手抄回来细读，后来逃难到山东时才得到一部王弼注释的《易经》，他日夜诵读。当时虽兵荒马乱，许衡仍坚持日读夜思，且身体力行。

南宋末年，许衡同众人一起逃难。他们从洛阳渡河经过河阳，当时正是炎热的夏天，烈日像火球一样炙烤着大地。众人由于长时间赶路而汗流浃背、口干舌燥。这时，一个人看到远处有棵梨树，立刻喊道："前面有梨树，大家快去摘梨来解渴。"众人一听，赶忙收拾东西去摘梨。可是许衡却没动。有个人奇怪地问："你为什么不去摘梨呢？"许衡问道："梨树的主人在吗？"众人都说："现在时局混乱，梨树的主人早就已经不在了，天气这么热，摘几个梨解渴也没什么大不了的，何必如此介意呢？"许衡认真地说："梨树虽然没有主人看管，难道我们自己的心也没有约束吗？我的心有约束，不是自己的东西，又没经主人允许，我是绝不会去偷的。别人丢失的东西即使十分微小我都不会去拿，因为这不符合道义。就像庭院里有棵果树，果子熟了掉到地上，受过教育的孩子连瞥都不会瞥一眼，何况是去捡它呢？人们因为受过教育，所以才会有美好的品德。"众人听后，纷纷感到很羞愧。

通过这个小小的事例，我们可以看出许衡不仅注重读书，而且重视身体力行。他认为要充分做到知行合一就需要通过自己的实践检验。实际上，许衡一生都在坚持这个规则，他强调知行合一，常说"纲常伦理，国家一日不可废，即使身居高位的人不履行，我们一般人也要履行"。强调实行正是以许衡为代表的元代北学最重要的特点。许衡不食无主之梨的典故，表明他从小就重视知识和实践的统一。

许衡在他三十四岁时，接触到了程朱理学，这是他一生学术道路的重要转折点。他感觉过去所学所教并未抓住主旨，对程朱理学到了入迷

tree in the distance and exclaimed, "A pear tree ahead! Let's go and pick some to quench our thirst." Upon hearing this, they dashed to pick pears after settling their belongings. But Xu Heng did not move. A man inquired, "Why don't you pick pears?" Xu replied, "Is the owner of the pear tree there?" Others answered, "The owner might have gone given the chaotic situation. It's so hot that picking a few pears to quench thirst is no big deal. Why do you bother?" Xu Heng replied seriously: "Although the pear tree is not under care of its owner, are we not bound by our own hearts? My heart is bound. It is not my own thing, and I will never steal it without its owner's permission. I will not take anything lost by others, even if it is small, because this is immoral. Just like a fruit tree in the courtyard, when ripened fruits fall to the ground, educated children will not even glance at them, let alone pick them up? Being educated gives us integrity and virtues." The others felt ashamed when they heard Xu Heng.

This example reflects that Xu Heng paid attention to both reading and practicing. Unity of knowledge and practice needs to be tested in daily practices. In fact, Xu Heng adhered to this rule all his life. He emphasized unity of knowledge and action, claiming that "A country should not abolish principles and ethics even one day. Even if people in high positions do not implement it, we ordinary people should implement it" .Focus on practice proves to be the most typical feature of the Northern School of Learning represented by Xu Heng in the Yuan Dynasty. The allusion that Xu Heng would not eat pears without the owner's permission shows that he emphasized unity of knowledge and practice since his childhood.

Xu Heng came into contact with Neo-Confucianism advocated by Masters Cheng Hao, Cheng Yi and Zhu Xi when he was 34 years old, a vital turning point in his academic career. He felt that what he had learned and taught in the past didn't possess the core, so he was fascinated by Neo-Confucianism. He once told his children that he worshiped *Commentaries on the Four Books* by Zhu Xi like the God. He believed that if he could understand this book, he would give up all other books. Xu Heng became an official in the Yuan Dynasty under conscription of the Emperor Kublai Khan after the dynasty was established. He served a long time as an officer in charge of the Imperial College, presided over education policy, and spared no effort in enlightening citizens via education. He promoted

的程度。他曾对自己的孩子说，他对朱熹的《四书集注》像神明一样相信，如果能明了此书，其他的书不学也罢。元朝建立后，在当时皇帝忽必烈的征召下，许衡入仕元朝。许衡长期担任国子监祭酒，主持教育工作，承宣教化，不遗余力。他大力发展程朱理学，使得理学在实际上获得了准官学的地位。后来许衡又负责制定历法的领导工作，为元朝制造了《授时历》。1281年，许衡在家乡病逝。

许衡承接两宋以来的儒学道统，推崇理学又力践躬行，为时人所折服。他在元代理学北方传授体系的建立过程中发挥了很大作用，明代大儒薛瑄称赞许衡是朱熹之后最重要的一个儒学人物。

the sort of Neo-Confucianism advocated by Masters Cheng Hao, Cheng Yi and Zhu Xi, which rendered Neo-Confucianism as de facto a quasi-official school. Later, he led in formulating a calendar, and created the *Shoushi Calendar* for the Yuan Dynasty. In 1281AD, Xu Heng died of illness in his hometown.

Xu Heng inherited Confucian orthodoxy during the Song dynasties, advocated Neo-Confucianism and practiced it, admired by his fellows. He played an indispensable role in promoting Neo-Confucianism in the northern teaching system of the Yuan Dynasty. Xue Xuan, a great Confucian in the Ming Dynasty, praised Xu Heng as the most important Confucian after Zhu Xi.

五、高风让国（朱载堉）

大家印象中的王子一般都是风度翩翩、锦衣玉食，过着无忧无虑的生活。中国古代有一位王子的经历却与一般的王子不同，他就是被人们称为布衣王子的朱载堉。一般人或许对他知之甚少，但他的确是一位了不起的人物。

高风让国（朱载堉）
Renouncing the Title of Prince（Zhu Zaiyu）

V. Renouncing the Title of Prince (Zhu Zaiyu)

Princes in our impression are generally elegant, well-dressed and living a carefree life. In ancient China, one prince's experience was different from that of ordinary princes. He was Zhu Zaiyu, who was called the Civilian Prince. The public may know little about him, but he was an impressive man.

As a prince of the Ming Dynasty, Zhu Zaiyu has been still an worldwide influential figure till now. He was born in Qinyang (formerly known as Huaiqing Mansion), Henan Province in 1536AD. His father Zhu Houwan, Prince Gong of Zheng, was a brother of the same generation of Emperor Jiajing of the Ming Dynasty. Zhu Houwan, a talented scholar, was humble and respectful to the wise and had a straightforward disposition. He dared to admonish Emperor Jiajing when the emperor was addicted to Daoism. He wrote to the emperor that it was inappropriate to do so, which angered the latter who ordered the imprisonment of the messenger sent by Zhu Houwan. Later, Zhu was falsely accused of rebellion due to conflicts between the royal families. Hence he was stripped of his title and escorted from his residence at Huaiqing Mansion to Fengyang, Anhui Province, where his family originated. At this time, his son Zhu Zaiyu was only 15 years old. The lad was furious that he could not save his father, so he moved out of the palace. He built an earthen house outside the palace, used wormwood as a mat, wore coarse clothes and ate simple fare, and waited for 19 years. During the time, Zhu Zaiyu did not get depressed or waste time because of family changes. Instead, he cheered up and devoted himself to learning of music, astronomy and the calendar. It was not until Emperor Longqing ascended the throne and Zhu Houwan was pardoned, that the father and son returned to their original residence together.

When his father died of illness in 1591AD, Zhu Zaiyu, as the eldest son, could have inherited the title of prince according to regulations of the Ming Dynasty. However, the son wrote to Emperor Wanli at that time, voluntarily renouncing the title to descendants of the clansman who framed his father. Officials pointed out that although Zhu Zaiyu gave up the title, there was no reason for the title to be inherited by other families. If Zhu Zaiyu didn't want

朱载堉是朱明王朝的王子，是直至今天仍具有世界影响力的人物。1536年，朱载堉出生在河南沁阳（旧时称怀庆府）。他的父亲郑恭王朱厚烷，是明朝嘉靖皇帝的同辈兄弟。朱厚烷才学过人，折节下士，而且秉性耿直。他敢于直谏，当时的嘉靖皇帝沉迷于道家，朱厚烷给皇帝上书直言这样做不妥。皇帝恼怒之余，下令囚禁朱厚烷派去的使者。因皇族之间的矛盾，朱厚烷被人诬告谋反。他因此被削夺爵位，从郑王府第怀庆府押送到朱氏老家安徽凤阳禁锢。此时朱载堉只有15岁，他气愤于自己无法救护父亲，因此从王宫中搬了出去。他在王宫外筑造土屋，以蒿草当席子，布衣蔬食，一年一年地等待着，就这样一直过了19年。在这19年里，朱载堉并没有因为家庭变故而一蹶不振、虚度光阴，反而振作起来潜心向学，一心钻研乐律、天文、历法等方面的知识。直到后来隆庆帝即位，朱厚烷才得以赦免，父子二人才一起回到原来的府第。

1591年，朱载堉的父亲朱厚烷病逝，因为朱载堉是家中长子，按照明朝的规定他本可以继承王位。但朱载堉却上书当时的万历皇帝，自愿放弃王位，将王位让给当年诬陷其父亲的族人的后代。有关官员提出，虽然朱载堉礼让王位，但是没有选择其他支系继承王位的道理；如果朱载堉不继承王位，应该由他的儿子继承。即便如此，朱载堉也不答应，执意要让出王位。在历经15年7次上奏请辞之后，1606年，万历皇帝才最终同意。当时朱载堉已经70岁，皇帝特地命人建造了"让国高风"的牌坊褒奖他。让出王位之后，朱载堉自称道人，潜心著书，过着普通学者的生活。

朱载堉自幼便聪慧过人，他一生以学问为主，著书立说。在音律、数学、历法等领域，朱载堉建树颇多，有几项成果更被列为世界第一，海内外学者予以高度评价，朱载堉也因此被誉为中国文艺复兴式的人物。

朱载堉对世界文化最大的贡献是创建了十二平均律，这是音乐学和音乐物理学的一大革命，也是世界科学史上的一大发明。他在总结前人乐律理论基础上，通过精密计算和科学实验，成功地发明了十二平均律，

to inherit the title, his son should do so. Even so, Zhu refused and insisted on renouncing the title. Eventually, Emperor Wanli agreed to Zhu Zaiyu's request in 1606AD after seven resignations in fifteen years. At that time, Zhu Zaiyu was 70 years old. The emperor ordered the construction of a memorial archway called "Renouncing the Title of Prince" to praise him. Zhu Zaiyu devoted himself to writing books and living the life of an ordinary scholar as he claimed to be a Daoist after renouncing the title.

Zhu Zaiyu was intelligent since he was young. All his life, he focused on learning and writing books. He made a difference in the fields of musicology, mathematics, and the calendar. Several achievements topped the world and won praise from scholars both at home and abroad. Therefore, he is still known as a key figure of the Chinese Renaissance.

Zhu Zaiyu's greatest contribution to the world culture was the idea of the twelve-tone equal temperament, a great revolution in musicology and music physics, and an impressive invention in the history of the world science. He invented the twelve-tone equal temperament through precise calculation and scientific experiments, and outlined its calculation in detail on the basis of summarizing previous music theories. This discovery was a major event in the history of music. The manufacture of modern musical instruments is based on the twelve-tone equal temperament. His findings were influenced by his father. He drew inspiration from his father's superb cognition of phonology.

In addition to his attainments in science, Zhu Zaiyu enjoyed profound views on Chinese traditional culture, manifested by a stone tablet called "Primeval Unity of Three Religions and Nine Schools" now preserved in the Shaolin Temple in Dengfeng, Henan Province. It can be seen from the eulogy on the upper part of the tablet that "Three Religions" here refers to Buddhism, Daoism and Confucianism. "Nine Schools" refers to the nine schools of thought in ancient China, namely, Mohist School, Agriculturist, Skilled Doctors, School of Logicians, Legalists, Eclectics, School of Positive and Negative Forces (Yin and Yang), Political Strategists, and Novelists. "Primeval Unity" means integrating the three religions and nine schools. In the middle of this tablet is a mixed painting of primeval unity drawn by Zhu Zaiyu. As a thought-provoking portrayal, this stunning picture includes Sakyamuni, founder of Buddhism; the

并详细概述了十二平均律的计算方法。这一发现是音乐史上的重大事件，现代乐器的制造都是用十二平均律来定音的。朱载堉的这些发现，受到了他父亲的影响，朱厚烷对音律学的认知给朱载堉很大的启发。

除了在科学方面的造诣，朱载堉对中国传统文化有着非常深刻的见解。现在保存在河南登封少林寺院内的"混元三教九流图赞碑"，就是最好的证明。从碑上部的赞词可知，这里的三教，指佛、道、儒三家，九流是中国古代九种学派，即墨、农、医、名、法、杂、阴阳、纵横、小说家，"混元"是说三教九流融为一体。此碑中部是一幅由朱载堉绘制的混元图。这是一幅发人深思的线刻画，它将佛教创始人释迦牟尼、儒教创始人孔子的侧视像、道教始祖老子的侧视像，一同绘制在这幅美丽的画卷中。这面碑刻内涵深邃，独具匠心，真正体现了儒、佛、道三教融为一体和九流同归之意。它表明了朱载堉对中国传统思想文化发展进程所做的概括和描绘。

明王朝对封王于各地的宗室人员控制甚严，如不许他们做官、考科举，不许他们与当地官员交往，不许他们从事工商业。在这种高压政策之下，明代的宗室成员难以施展才智为社会做出贡献，形成一个坐食岁禄的寄生阶层。朱载堉虽然出身宗室，但却立志学术，成就非凡，而且他道德高尚、淡泊名利。因此，人们亲切地称他为"布衣王子"。

side view of Confucius, founder of Confucianism; and a side view of Laozi, founder of Daoism. This stele, with profound connotation and originality, reflects the integration of Confucianism, Buddhism and Daoism and the unity of the nine schools. It presents the painter's summary and description of the growth of Chinese traditional ideology and culture.

The Ming Dynasty exerted strict control over imperial family members who were granted the title of prince in different feudatories. For example, they were not allowed to be officials, take imperial examinations, associate with local officials, or engage in industry and commerce. Under this high-pressure policy, royal members of the Ming Dynasty made it impossible to exert their princes' talents and make a difference to the society. Thus they formed a parasitic class of eating without toiling. Zhu Zaiyu set up his mind to learn and earned extraordinary achievements despite his royal origin. Moreover, he was moral and indifferent to fame and wealth. Thus, he won the affectionate reputation of the title—"Civilian Prince".

六、万金济黉（康百万）

人世间的事情变化无常，俗话说："三十年河东，三十年河西。"在中国古代社会，就每一个家族而言，无论是富还是贵，"富不过三代""三世而不衰者鲜"，富或贵能一直延续超过三代的情况并不多见。然而，河南的康百万家族，却一连富了12代，前后延续竟有400多年，这一个案令人惊奇，在中国历史上极其少见。尤为可贵的是，康百万家族非常重视教育和地方慈善事业，留下了"万金济黉"的典故。

万金济黉（康百万）

Granting Ten Thousand in Gold to Build Schools（The Millionaire Kang Family）

VI. Granting Ten Thousand in Gold to Build Schools (The Millionaire Kang Family)

The future is unpredictable. As a saying goes, "Fortune would work to the converse after 30 years." In ancient Chinese society, for every family, whether rich or royal, "Few families could be wealthy for three generations in a row" and "Three generations without decline are rare". It is rare for families to maintain fortune or high status for over three generations. However, "the Millionaire Kang Family of Henan" is an exception. This family was rich for 12 generations in a row in a time span of over 400 years. This surprising case was unusual in Chinese history. What is worth noting is that the Kang Family stressed education and local charities, leaving behind the idiom—"Granting Ten Thousand in Gold to Build Schools".

The Millionaire Kang Family was located in Kangdian village, Kangdian Town, west of Gongyi City, Henan Province. The Kang family moved there from Shanxi in the early Ming Dynasty. The first ancestor of the family was Kang Shouxin. By the time of the sixth generation Kang Shaojing, the Kang family had amassed large areas of land and wedged into the ranks of the landlord class. Since then, the family had flourished and prospered. In history, merchants from Shanxi and Huizhou areas mostly traveled to other cities and tried their luck in business. In contrast, the Kang family focused more on land management. They grew grain and cotton and earned profits from exporting goods. Kang Dayong, the 12th generation descendant of the family, endeavored to establish presence in other regions by accumulated financial might. The family built their own ships and started shipping. They always purchased a piece of land first, then monopolized business even when they traveled to thousands of miles away, which reflected how they valued land. Kang's fleet covered a wide range, reaching Beijing in the north, Yangzhou in the south, and covering Shaanxi, Shanxi, Shandong, Jiangsu and other regions nearby. Their business thrived. Kang Dayong also built a business headquarter in Lanshui County, Shandong Province. His business laid the foundation for the family's trade.

Kang Yingkui, Kang Dayong's grandson, the 14th generation descendant, soared to the prime representative of his family business. He built the family's

康百万家族位于河南省巩义市城西的康店镇康店村，这里的康家是明朝初年从山西迁来的，一世祖是康守信。到第六世康绍敬时，康家已拥有大片土地，步入地主阶级行列。从此，人丁兴旺，家运昌盛。历史上的晋商、徽商多奔走他乡，在商海闯荡，相比而言，康家人更重视土地经营，他们自己种粮食、种棉花，外销盈利。随着财力的扩大，到十二世康大勇时，便开始跨区经营，他们自己造船搞起了航运。但即使远到千里之外，康家也总是要先买一块地，再垄断经营，有着浓厚的"农本"思想。康家的船队活动范围很大，北到北京，南达扬州，附近遍及陕西、山西、山东、江苏等地区。生意也越做越大，康大勇还在山东兰水县建了栈房。康大勇的经营，奠定了康家经商的基础。

到康大勇的孙子十四世康应魁时，他把家业做到了极致，在洛河岸边建起了自家的造船厂，在山东日照等地设立了新栈房，购置了地产。在陕西，康家掌控了布匹批发市场，并在那里购置土地种植棉花，保证低成本原料的供应。康家还从官方拿到了一份长达10年的军需品订单。这使得康家的财力和势力范围进一步扩大。康应魁是康家历史上一个了不起的人物，在他掌管期间，康家进入鼎盛时期，成为无与伦比的中原豪富之家。巩义民间有句顺口溜说："河里行的康家船，岸上种的康家田，路上跑的康家马，栈里借的康家钱。"康应魁被称为"活财神"，是康家经商最成功的人，也是中国封建时代地主兼大商人的杰出代表。

俗话说，"发财容易，守财难"，为何康氏家族能够守住财富呢？因为康氏家族非常重视教育，形成了一套严格的家训家规，并且每个人都要严格遵守，这也是康氏家族能够保持长盛不衰的原因。康应魁在发展商业的同时，不忘祖辈的教诲，发展了其家族的文化。他以家族家训修身，不仅重视家族教育，而且懂得泽被乡里。道光八年（公元1828年），康应魁花费了大量金银，独资修筑了县城里规格庞大、雕梁画栋的巩县五圣庙，供奉了儒家五圣。同年，他又独资修建成巩县的高级学校，使全县的人都能有上学受教育的地方。康应魁品德高尚、造福乡里，因此

own shipyard on the bank of Luohe River, set up new centers in Rizhao, Shandong Province, and purchased real estate. In Shaanxi Province, the family controlled the wholesale market of cloth and purchased land there to plant cotton to ensure supply of low-cost raw materials. The family also secured a 10-year order of military supplies from the government. This further added glory to the financial resources and sphere of influence of the Kang family. Kang Yingkui was an impressive figure in the history of his family. During his management, the Kang family entered its heyday and became an affluent family in the Central Plains, second to none. A folk verse in Gongyi says, "Boats in the river come from the Kang family, fields on the bank belong to the Kang family, horses on the road are from the Kang family, and money borrowed from headquarters flow from the Kang family." Kang Yingkui was known as the "Living God of Wealth". He was a role model of businessmen of the Kang family and an outstanding representative of landlords and businessmen in the feudal era of China.

As a saying goes, "Easy to get rich, hard to keep the wealth." How could the Kang family keep it? Because the family valued education. It formed a set of strict disciplines and rules, and everyone was expected to abide by them, which was also the reason why the family could maintain its prosperity. While doing business, Kang Yingkui did not forget the teachings of his ancestors and he nurtured culture of his family. He cultivated himself with family disciplines and rules. He not only valued family education, but also brought benefits to villagers in the hometown. He built a magnificent temple with carved beams in Gongxian County (Gongyi County) dedicated to the five saints of Confucianism by spending a large amount of money in 1828AD (the eighth year of Emperor Daoguang's reign). In the same year, he also built a senior school in Gongxian County, so that residents in the whole county could be educated. Because of his noble morals and good deeds, Kang Yingkui was loved by the locals. Residents in his hometown sponsored a plaque entitled "Granting Ten Thousand in Gold to Build Schools" to honor his efforts.

However, the Kang family declined from its prime beginning with the 15th generation. A donation of a million silver taels from the family won the fame of the designation—"The Millionaire Kang Family" but rendered its decline under the management of Kang Hongyou in the family's 17th generation. The famous

得到百姓的爱戴。为了感谢他修建学校，大家合资铸造了"万金济黉"的匾额赠予他。

不过，康家自十五世以后，已由盛转衰。尤其是到十七世康鸿猷掌门期间，虽然赢得了"康百万"的美名，却换来了家业的败落。"康百万"这个称谓，据说是慈禧太后封赐的。光绪二十七年（公元1901年），慈禧太后一行从西安返回京城途中，路经巩县康店村南的黑石关行宫。该行宫不是地方官府所建，而是康鸿猷拿出康家大笔钱财独资修建的。此时，康鸿猷又献给慈禧太后白银100万两。慈禧顺便说了一句："没承想，这山沟里还有百万之家"。光绪二十九年（公元1903年），康家得到了一块朝廷赐给的金匾，上写"神州甲富康百万"。康鸿猷斥巨资为康家挣得了一个虚名——"康百万"！从此以后，"康百万"这个封号就流传开了，也使得康百万庄园的名声大振。可是康家大业也由此走向衰败。

康氏家族经营四百多年，建造了一个依山傍水、错落有致、气势宏伟的大庄园。如今，已历经数百年风雨沧桑的康百万庄园，依然矗立在伊洛河岸边。透过这些青瓦高墙，我们依稀能够感知康氏家族曾经的辉煌。

北宋时期，中原地区依然是全国的政治、文化中心。"杯酒释兵权"是本书中最后一个发生在河南的重要政治典故，反映了中国古人在国家治理上高明的政治智慧。此后，中国的政治、经济中心逐渐从中原地区转移出去。尽管相比从前中原地区的盛景不再，但是在文化方面中原地区依然拥有举足轻重的地位。"程门立雪""许衡不食无主之梨""高风让国"都是在理学思想的浸润下出现的故事，在儒学发展史和中国教育史上都有着重要的意义。"精忠报国"是中华民族爱国主义的一面旗帜，"万金济黉"更是中原地区人们一贯重视教育的体现。这些都是在厚重的中原文化沃土中孕育出来的经典故事，被后世传扬不衰，影响深远。

designation of the family is said to have been granted by Empress Dowager Cixi. In the twenty-seventh year of Guangxu (1901 AD), the Empress Dowager Cixi and her party passed by the Heishiguan Palace in the south of Kangdian Village, Gongxian County on their way back to the capital from Xi'an. The palace was not built by the local government but solely by Kang Hongyou with a large sum of money from his family. At this time, Kang Hongyou also presented one million taels of silver (50,000 kilograms) to the Empress Dowager. Cixi said casually, "I never thought there was a millionaire in this remote area." Later the Kang family received a gold plaque from the imperial court, which read "The Millionaire Kang Family in China" in 1903AD (the 29th year of Emperor Guangxu's reign). Kang Hongyou spent millions of silver to earn an inflated reputation for his family—The Millionaire Kang Family! From then on, the title gained popularity, which also rendered the manor of the Kang family more famous. However, the great cause of the Kang family had also declined since that time.

It took the Kang family over 400 years to build a Grand Manor, neat, magnificent and situated at the foot of a hill and beside a river. Today, the manor still stands on the bank of the Yiluo River after hundreds of years of vicissitudes. We can still have a glimpse of the past glory of the Kang family through the manor's green tiles and high walls.

The Central Plains was still the political and cultural core of China during the Northern Song Dynasty. "Releasing the Military Power by Wining and Dining", the last vital political allusion in this book that occurred in Henan, reflects brilliant political wisdom of ancient Chinese in national governance. Since then, China's political and economic center had gradually shifted away from the Central Plains. Although the Central Plains no longer enjoys the same level of prosperity as in the past, it still plays a decisive role in culture. "Standing in the Snow to Wait upon Master Cheng", "Xu Heng Wouldn't Eat Pears Without the Owner's Permission", "Renouncing the Title of Prince" all appear under the effects of Neo-Confucianism, which is of great significance in the history of Confucianism and Chinese education. "Serve the Country Faithfully" acts as a banner of Chinese patriotism. "Granting Ten Thousand in Gold to Build Schools" embodies the truth that people in the Central Plains always highlighted education. These are classic blossoms bred in fertile soil of Central Plains' culture, which have been spread by later generations and exerted a far-reaching impact.

附录：中国历史年代简表

Appendix: A Brief Chronology of Chinese History

中国历史年代简表
A Brief Chronology of Chinese History

五帝时代 Period of the Five Legendary Rulers c. 2600 BC–c. 2070 BC	黄帝 Huangdi (Yellow Emperor)	
	颛顼 Zhuanxu	
	帝喾 Diku (Emperor Ku)	
	尧 Yao	
	舜 Shun	
夏 Xia Dynasty	c. 2070 BC–c. 1600 BC	
商 Shang Dynasty	c. 1600 BC–c. 1046 BC	
西周 Western Zhou Dynasty	c. 1046 BC–c. 771 BC	
东周 Eastern Zhou Dynasty 770 BC–256 BC	春秋 Spring and Autumn Period	770 BC–476 BC
	战国 Warring States Period	475 BC–221 BC
秦 Qin Dynasty	221 BC–206 BC	
汉 Han Dynasty 206 BC–220 AD	西汉 Western Han	206 BC–25 AD
	东汉 Eastern Han	25 AD–220 AD
三国 Three Kingdoms 220 AD–280 AD	魏 Wei	220 AD–265 AD
	蜀汉 Shu Han	221 AD–263 AD
	吴 Wu	222 AD–280 AD
晋 Jin Dynasty 265 AD–420 AD	西晋 Western Jin	265 AD–317 AD
	东晋 Eastern Jin	317 AD–420 AD

续表 Continued Table

南北朝 Southern and Northern Dynasties 420 AD-589 AD	南朝 Southern Dynasties	宋 Song	420 AD-479 AD
		齐 Qi	479 AD-502 AD
		梁 Liang	502 AD-557 AD
		陈 Chen	557 AD-589 AD
	北朝 Northern Dynasties	北魏 Northern Wei	386 AD-534 AD
		东魏 Eastern Wei	534 AD-550 AD
		北齐 Northern Qi	550 AD-577 AD
		西魏 Western Wei	535 AD-556 AD
		北周 Northern Zhou	557 AD-581 AD
隋 Sui Dynasty		581 AD-618 AD	
唐 Tang Dynasty		618 AD-907 AD	
五代十国 Five Dynasties and Ten States	五代 Five Dynasties 907 AD-960 AD	后梁 Later Liang	907 AD-923 AD
		后唐 Later Tang	923 AD-936 AD
		后晋 Later Jin	936 AD-947 AD
		后汉 Later Han	947 AD-950 AD
		后周 Later Zhou	951 AD-960 AD
	十国 Ten States 902 AD-979 AD	北汉 Northern Han	951 AD-979 AD
		吴 Wu	902 AD-937 AD
		吴越 Wuyue	907 AD-978 AD
		闽 Min	909 AD-945 AD
		南汉 Southern Han	917 AD-971 AD
		荆南(又称"南平") Jingnan (Nanping)	924 AD-963 AD
		楚 Chu	927 AD-951 AD
		南唐 Southern Tang	937 AD-975 AD
		前蜀 Former Shu	907 AD-925 AD
		后蜀 Later Shu	934 AD-965 AD

续表 Continued Table

宋 Song Dynasty 960 AD-1279 AD	北宋 Northern Song	960 AD-1127 AD
	南宋 Southern Song	1127 AD-1279 AD
辽 Liao (契丹 Qidan/Khitan)	907 AD-1125 AD	
西夏 Xixia (Tangut)	1038 AD-1227 AD	
金 Jin	1115 AD-1234 AD	
元 Yuan Dynasty	1206 AD-1368 AD	
明 Ming Dynasty	1368 AD-1644 AD	
清 Qing Dynasty	1616 AD-1911 AD	
中华民国 Republic of China	1912 AD-1949 AD	
中华人民共和国 People's Republic of China	1949 AD-